Top 25 locator map
(continues on inside
back cover)
◄——

D1321700

# CityPack
# Seattle *Top 25*

**SUZANNE TEDESKO**

If you have any comments
or suggestions for this guide
you can contact the editor at
*Citypack@theAA.com*

**AA Publishing**
Find out more about AA Publishing and the
wide range of services the AA provides by
visiting our website at *www.theAA.com*

# About This Book

### ORGANIZATION

This guide is divided into six sections:
- Planning Ahead, Getting There
- Living Seattle—Seattle Now, Seattle Then, Time to Shop, Out and About, Walks, Seattle by Night
- Seattle's Top 25 Sights
- Seattle's Best—best of the rest
- Where To—detailed listings of restaurants, hotels, shops and nightlife
- Travel Facts—practical information

In addition, easy-to-read side panels provide extra facts and snippets, highlights of places to visit and invaluable practical advice.

The colors of the tabs on the page corners match the colors of the triangles aligned with the chapter names on the contents page opposite.

### MAPS

**The fold-out map** in the wallet at the back of this book is a comprehensive street plan of Seattle. The first (or only) grid reference given for each attraction refers to this map. **The Top 25 locator map** found on the inside front and back covers of the book itself is for quick reference. It shows the Top 25 Sights, described on pages 26–50, which are clearly plotted by number (**1**–**25**, not page number) across the city. The second map reference given for the Top 25 Sights refers to this map.

# Contents

# Planning Ahead

## WHEN TO GO

The weather may be best in summer, but Seattle is a year-round destination as the focal point for arts in the Pacific Northwest. Ringed by ski resorts, Seattle attracts winter sports enthusiasts, and sports fans visit during the baseball season. At any time of year be sure to arrive with a hotel reservation no matter.

### TIME

Seattle is on Pacific Standard Time, three hours behind New York, eight hours behind the UK.

## AVERAGE DAILY MAXIMUM TEMPERATURES

| JAN | FEB | MAR | APR | MAY | JUN | JUL | AUG | SEP | OCT | NOV | DEC |
|-----|-----|-----|-----|-----|-----|-----|-----|-----|-----|-----|-----|
| 45°F | 50°F | 53°F | 59°F | 66°F | 70°F | 76°F | 75°F | 69°F | 62°F | 51°F | 47°F |
| 7°C | 10°C | 12°C | 13°C | 19°C | 21°C | 24°C | 24°C | 20°C | 16°C | 10°C | 8°C |

**Spring** (March to May) brings a flurry of bulbs and flowering trees; weather can be unsettled.

**Summer** (June to August) is sunny and clear, with cool nights. Plan to dress in layers.

**Fall** (September to November) is often lovely, particularly September, with rainfall averaging 1.88in (5cm).

**Winter** (December to February) rarely brings snow to the city, although the Cascades and Olympic Mountains receive vast quantities. November to January are the rainiest months.

## WHAT'S ON

**January** *Chinese and Vietnamese New Year's Celebration.*

**February** *Fat Tuesday:* Mardi Gras celebration in Pioneer Square.

**March** *Imagination Celebration/Art Festival for Kids. Seattle Fringe Festival.*

**April** *Cherry Blossom and Japanese Cultural Festival.*

**May** *Opening Day of Yachting Season* (first Saturday). *International Children's Theater Festival:* Performances by groups around the world. *University Street Fair.*

*Northwest Folklife Festival:* The largest in the country. *Pike Place Market Festival. Seattle International Film Festival.*

**June** *Fremont Solstice Parade and Celebration* (21 Jun): A celebration of the longest day. *Fremont Arts and Crafts Fair. Out to Lunch Summer:* Downtown concerts. *Summer Nights on the Pier:* Concert series.

**July** *Fourth of July. Lake Union Wooden Boat Festival. Caribbean Festival–A Taste of Soul. Chinatown International*

*District Summer Festival. Bite of Seattle Food Fest. Pacific Northwest Arts and Crafts Fair. Seafair:* Races on water featuring everything from milk-carton derbies and hydrofoil heats plus tribal pow-wows and more.

**September** *Bambershoot:* Festival of music, visual arts and crafts.

**October** *Northwest bookfest:* Literary festival.

**December** *Christmas Ship:* Brightly lit vessels make the rounds of the beaches with choirs aboard who sing carols to people on the shore.

## SEATTLE ONLINE

**www.seeseattle.org**
The Seattle-King County Visitors Bureau website. Listings and a calendar of events.

**http://seattle.citysearch.com**
Comprehensive city guide with travel, hotels, dining and entertainment listings, and a readers' rating system. Local weather information with five-day forecasts and satellite photographs.

**www.nwsource,com**
Pacific Northwest arts and entertainment guide, service of Seattle's two daily newspapers, with links to hotels, tours, transportation, local weather, the outdoors and classified ads.

**http://tripplanner.metrokc.gov**
Seattle Metro helps you plan bus transportation from point A to B. Provides route numbers, stop locations, schedules and next-bus-out information.

**www.wsdot.wa.gov/ferries**
Official Washington State ferry website, with schedule and fare information for Bainbridge, Vashon & Whidbey islands, the Kitsap Peninsula, the San Juan Islands, and Victoria, British Columbia.

**www.graylineofseattle.com**
Bus service between Sea-Tac airport and downtown, plus bus tours.

**www.seattlehotelrooms.com**
Seattle area hotels reviewed and listed by location. Discounted online reservations.

**www.weather.com**
Weather information by city and Zip code; current conditions, 10-day forecast, weather alerts and satellite photographs.

**www.Amtrak.com**
Route, fare and schedule information for Amtrak rail service.

## GOOD TRAVEL SITES

**www.fodors.com**
A complete travel-planning site. Research prices and weather; book air tickets, cars and rooms; pose questions to fellow travelers; and find links to other sites.

**www.wamaps.com**
Maps from all over the state of Washington.

**www.access.wa.gov**
Washington State's home page provides everything you need to know to venture further afield.

## CYBERCAFÉS

**CapitolHill.net**
➕ D4  ✉ 216 Broadway E  ☎ 206/860–6858  🕐 Daily 8am–midnight  💵 $.10 per minute

**The Online Coffee Company**
➕ E3  ✉ 1111 1st Avenue  ☎ 206/381–1911  🕐 Mon–Fri 7am–midnight, Sat–Sun 9am–midnight  💵 $.12 per minute

**Aurafice Internet & Coffee Bar**
➕ D4  ✉ 616 Pine Street E  ☎ 206/860–9977  🕐 Sun–Thu 8am–midnight, Fri–Sat 8am–2am  💵 $.50 per minute

# Getting There

## ENTRY REQUIREMENTS

Visitors from outside the US must show a passport valid for at least six months. Most UK citizens and visitors from other countries belonging to the Visa Waiver Program can enter without a visa, but you must have a return or onward ticket. For further details go online at www.usembassy.org.uk

## MONEY

The unit of currency is the dollar (= 100 cents). Bills (notes) come in denominations of $1, $5, $10, $20, $50 and $100; coins are 25¢ (a quarter), 10¢ (a dime), 5¢ (a nickel) and 1¢ (a penny).

$5

$10

$50

$100

## ARRIVING

Sea-Tac International Airport is 15 miles (24km) south of downtown Seattle. Flights from New York take 5–6 hours, from LA 2–3 hours and from London about 11 hours. Upon arrival, look for the large airport maps located near escalators, or get help from an airport volunteer.

### FROM SEA-TAC INTERNATIONAL AIRPORT

For airport information ☎ 206/433–5388. An information desk near baggage claim provides current details on ground transportation. There are a variety of ways to get downtown. Travel time is 30 minutes or more, depending on transportation mode and traffic conditions.

Grayline Airport Express (☎ 206/626–6088) runs buses to downtown hotels every half hour from 5am–11pm; cost is $7.50. Shuttle Express (☎ 425/981–7000) runs a 24-hour, door-to-door service between the airport and various locations; cost is about $18. Metro Transit buses to downtown leave from the baggage-claim level, outside door 6; exact change is required and costs between $1.25 and $2 one way (☎ 206/553–3000, 800/542–7876 or log on to the website, ► 5).

Taxis pick up passengers on the third floor of the parking garage, across from the Main Terminal. Fares are around $25–$30 to downtown. Nine rental companies have information counters on the baggage-claim level, and five offer car pick-up and drop-off on the first floor of the airport garage across from the Main Terminal.

### ARRIVING BY BUS

Greyhound (☎ 800/231–2222) buses arrive and leave from Seattle's Greyhound Terminal downtown at 811 Stewart Street. Green Tortoise Alternative Travel (☎ 800/867–8647) run twice-weekly between Seattle and Los Angeles.

### ARRIVING BY CAR

If you arrive by car you will enter the city via I–5. Downtown exits are Union Street (for City Center) and James Street (for Pioneer Square). If arriving via I–90 from the east you will cross the Lake Washington floating bridge; from there follow signs to I–5 north for downtown exits.

### ARRIVING BY TRAIN

Amtrak trains (☎ 800/872–7245) arrive at King Street Station at 3rd and Jackson, between Pioneer Square and the International District. The journey from LA takes about 35 hours. From New York you must change trains in Chicago (NY–Chicago 18–19 hours, Chicago–Seattle 46 hours).

### GETTING AROUND

Seattle's Metro Transit offers bus service throughout greater Seattle; timetables are available at many locations around town. Riding the bus in downtown is free between 6am and 7pm in Seattle's free-ride zone, except on the Waterfront Streetcar. Fares vary during peak hours (Mon–Fri 6–9am and 3–6pm) and non-peak hours. Adults pay $1.50 for one-zone and $2 for two-zone peak-hour trips, and $1.25 for non-peak trips. Exact change is required. A Visitor's Pass, available online and at Metro Customer Service offices, provides one-day unlimited travel on all Metro buses for $5.

The Monorail between downtown Westlake Center and Seattle Center (➤ 37) takes only 90 seconds. Trains run every 15 minutes; weekdays 7.30am–11pm and week-ends 9am–11pm. Adult tickets cost $1.25 per ride and can be purchased on the 3rd floor of Westlake Center and at Seattle Center beneath the Space Needle. Taxis are expensive—get one at your hotel or call for a radio-dispatched cab. For more getting around information ➤ 91–92.

### DRIVING IN SEATTLE

Slow-moving traffic and even gridlock is common on Interstate 5, Seattle's only freeway. Avenues and streets may have either names or numbers, but virtually all have helpful directional designations (NE, SW). Downtown Seattle has both on-street metered parking and garages and lots. Most meters cost $.25 per 15 minutes with a two-hour limit—and meter maids are vigilant.

### VISITORS WITH DISABILITIES

Downtown Seattle streets, especially those running east to west, can be difficult for travelers with a disability because of the city's steep hills. Streets and public buildings are required to have ramps, and some neighborhoods are level and evenly paved. Most of the city's buses have wheelchair lifts and designated space on the bus. For more information check the websites for Mobility International USA (www.miusa.org) and Access-Able Travel Source (www.access-able.com). There is 24-hour TTY operator service ☎ 800/855–1155.

# Living
# Seattle

# Seattle Now

Above: *Jogging on Alki Beach Park, West Seattle*

Named after the Indian chief, Sealth, who greeted early settlers, Seattle's youth, its immigrant population and its dazzling natural surroundings have shaped the character of this lively city of about 570,000 close to the Canadian border. The Cascade Mountains rise to the east, dominated by snowcapped Mt. Baker, Glacier Peak and the grandest volcano of them all—rising to 14,410ft (4,393m)—Mt. Rainier. To the west lies the rugged Olympic Range. Everywhere you look there's water—freshwater lakes, canals and saltwater Puget (PEW-jet) Sound. It's no wonder that Seattle claims more boats per capita than any other place in the US.

## GREATER SEATTLE

• These days, when people say Seattle, they no longer refer only to downtown and the neighborhoods within the city limits (➤ 57) but also to the greater metropolitan area, whose population now exceeds three million. Many residents live in the burgeoning area east of Lake Washington. Known as the "Eastside," this area, which includes Bellevue, Mercer Island, Redmond, Kirkland, Bothell and Issaquah, has experienced phenomenal growth as increasing numbers of high-tech companies located their offices and factories there, led by Miscrosoft, which built its sprawling campus in Redmond. Open space that was once forest or farmland was purchased for commercial and residential expansion.

### BILL GATES

● Seattle's best-known man has for several years been among the world's richest, with a net worth estimated at around $29 billion. Born in 1956, Bill Gates attended the city's most prestigious private school. Later he and school chum Paul Allen founded Microsoft, the world's most successful software company, which still has its world headquarters in Seattle's eastside at Redmond.

Above: *Seattle Waterfront*

Early pioneers built their homes along the shores of Elliott Bay on Puget Sound, site of today's downtown, and named their new community after the Native American chief who greeted the first settlers. As the town developed, its waterways and hilly terrain created natural barriers that divided the area into separate districts, each with its unique flavor. Seattle today is a city of thriving neighborhoods, dubbed by some as "urban villages."

Forty years ago, Seattle was a backwater—a company town with Scandinavian roots whose fortunes rose and fell on the wings of Boeing. Dramatic cultural and physical changes began in the 1970s in the wake of a Boeing recession. Thereafter, city fathers vowed to diversify the local economy. Voters elected a progressive new mayor and before long, a new civic vitality and can-do spirit began to stem the exodus of creative people. The new administration launched two popular festivals—the Northwest Folklife and the Bumbershoot—and introduced an ordinance that began to bring public art to every neighborhood, a process that continues today. Seattle's future was assured when two

hometown boys, Bill Gates and Paul Allen, founded a software company called Microsoft. Later, Starbucks opened its first coffee shop and sparked a craze for high-end coffee that has taken over every corner of the US. High-tech companies like Nintendo and online bookseller Amazon.com established themselves here. The area was becoming a major player in medical research, as the Fred Hutchinson Cancer Research Center performed more bone marrow transplants here than anywhere else in the US.

In 1989 Seattle was thought to be America's most livable city. Over the next decade, it garnered awards for everything from environmental consciousness to its emergency medical response system. When grunge music emerged from underground and garage bands like Nirvana drew international attention to the Seattle Sound, the city made its place on the world map of pop music.

The 1990s were Seattle's Gilded Age. The thriving economy provided jobs of all kinds and the population swelled and grew increasingly wealthy. The city was now a cultural mix, with

## THE "R" WORD

● Comedian Jerry Seinfeld once called Seattle "a moisturizing pad disguised as a city." But the local reputation for rainfall is largely undeserved. Annual precipitation averages 37–38in (95cm)—less than Boston, New York or Miami. What's misleading is how often it rains. There are many days and periods of on-again, off-again drizzle, yet, although it can be dark and gloomy one minute, it can be sparkling the next. And when Seattle sparkles, life doesn't get much better.

ethnic minorities accounting for 32 percent of the population. A strong Asian community spawned a sizable number of Asian restaurants and markets and inspired an aesthetic reminiscent of Japan's. Wealth created greater fashion-consciousness and sophistication. Gleaming new office towers competed for airspace, while condominiums, trendy cafés, restaurants and boutiques transformed downtown and the waterfront, and gentrified Belltown and Fremont. Many beneficiaries of the new prosperity,

Far Left: *Seattle Art Msueum*
Left: *Hing Hay Park' in Seattle's International District*
Above: *Reflections in Seattle*

### THE INVISIBLE THRONG

• A famous speech by Chief Sealth reminds us of the area's original inhabitants: "And when the last Red Man shall have perished…these shores will swarm with the invisible dead of my tribe, and when your children's children think themselves alone in the field, the store, the shop, upon the highway, or in the silence of the pathless woods, they will not be alone…At night when the streets of your cities and villages are silent and you think them deserted, they will throng with the returning hosts that once filled them and still love this beautiful land. The White Man will never be alone."

### THE GREAT OUTDOORS

• Wilderness areas are nearby and easily accessible. Outdoor enthusiasts flock to the region's forests, mountains and waterways to hike, ski, kayak or just get away from the city. Those that don't go away, go outside anyway—to garden, to take a ride on a bike trail or to play soccer in the park.

13

Above: Hammering Man
*statue*

including the so-called "Microsoft millionaires"—employees who had grown rich on stock options that were often part of the company's compensation packages—directed their philanthropy toward the city's cultural institutions.

As the millennium neared its close, traffic congestion ranked third worst in the nation; housing prices soared, and schools were over-enrolled. Development pushed the poor out of their old neighborhoods, and the numbers of homeless swelled. On the business front, Eastside companies were having morale problems. Dot.com fever was coming face-to-face with economic reality, and many companies went bankrupt. After the September 2001 terrorist attacks Boeing—already suffering from increased competition—declined as airplane

## SEATTLE STYLE

• Seattle is informal—the watchwords are "casual" and "comfortable." Even in theaters and restaurants, slacks and sweaters are acceptable for both men and women. Locals have a reputation for being both sophisticated and friendly, progressive yet polite. Environmental awareness runs high—smoking is prohibited in public buildings.

orders disappeared when Americans stopped traveling. By spring 2003, the Seattle area had the third highest unemployment in the nation.

Oddly enough, to walk the streets of Seattle, you'd never know it: The city feels vibrant. Two spanking new sports stadiums dominate the south Seattle skyline. The Seattle Opera and the Pacific Northwest Ballet have moved into impressive new halls at Seattle Center. Other municipal improvements that were on the drawing board when the city was flush are currently under construction, including a bold central library and a new city hall. An Olympic Sculpture Park (8.5-acre/4-ha sculpture garden) is planned for a 2004 opening on the city's largest tract of undeveloped waterfront. As for Seattle's unemployed, many are simplifying their lifestyle and taking pay cuts rather than leave the area. And many restaurants and small businesses are trying to ride out the hard times. Seattleites take things in stride—just as they do the weather. So welcome to the land of optimism and fresh starts. Pack your opera glasses and walking shoes, bring an umbrella, and prepare to do Seattle like a native.

Left: *Relaxing in Fremont*
Right: *Sailing in Elliott Bay*

## SEATTLE FIRSTS

- Gas station (1907).
- Public golf course in the US (1915).
- US general strike (1919; ► 17).
- Circumnavigational flight (1924).
- Woman mayor of a major American city (Bertha Landes; 1926).
- Water skis (1928).
- Concrete "floating " bridge (1939).
- Full-scale commercial monorail (1962).
- Covered shopping mall (1950).

# Seattle Then

## CHIEF SEALTH

Sealth was born in 1786 on Blake Island. In 1792, the young boy watched "the great canoe with giant white wings"—Captain Vancouver's brig—sail into Puget Sound. In his 20s he became leader of the Suquamish, Duwamish and allied bands, and became a friend to white settlers. One, the pioneer Arthur Denny, suggested changing the settlement's name from Alki to Sealth which, being difficult for whites to pronounce, was soon corrupted to Seattle. Preceeding the Indian War of 1856, Governor Isaac Stevens drafted a settlement promising the native tribes payments and reservation lands. Fearing his people's ways would disappear in the face of the growing number of settlers, Sealth reluctantly signed.

**1792** British Captain George Vancouver and his lieutenant, Peter Puget, explore the "inland sea," which Vancouver names Puget Sound.

**1851** David Denny, John Low and Lee Terry reach Alki Point and dub their colony "New York–Alki."

**1852** Pioneers move the settlement across Elliott Bay to what is now Pioneer Square.

**1853** Henry Yesler begins operating a steam sawmill, establishing the timber industry. President Fillmore signs an act creating the Washington Territory. (Washington achieves statehood in 1889.)

**1856** The so-called "Indian War": US battle sloop *Decatur* fires into downtown to root out native peoples, who burn the settlement.

**1869** The city is incorporated and passes its first public ordinance—a law against drunkenness.

**1889** The Great Seattle Fire causes damage exceeding $10 million.

**1893** James Hill's Great Northern Railroad reaches its western terminus, Seattle.

From left to right:
*A statue of Chief Seattle in Tilikum Place recalls the Native American whose name was given to the city; Bertha Landes, Seattle's first woman mayor, elected in 1926; Native American art displayed in the Daybreak Star Art Centre; the 42-story Smith Tower under construction—it was completed in 1914; statue of Lenin in front of the Fremont Hemp Co in Fremont—the statue was was rescued from Russia after the collapse of the Soviet system*

**1897** The ship Portland steams into Seattle carrying "a ton of gold" and triggers the Klondike Gold Rush.

**1909** The construction of Lake Washington Ship Canal begins, ending in 1917.

**1919** The Seattle General Strike, 60,000 workers walk off the job.

**1940** The Lake Washington Floating Bridge links Seattle with Eastside communities.

**1941** The US enters World War II. Workers flood Seattle to work in the shipyards and elsewhere.

**1949** An earthquake measuring 7.2 on the Richter scale strikes the area.

**1980** Mount St. Helens erupts, showering ash over Seattle, 100 miles (161km) away.

**1999** The World Trade Organization meets in Seattle. Protesters take to the streets.

**2001** An earthquake measuring 6.8 on the Richter scale rocks Seattle.

**2002** Seattle voters approve new monorail line linking Ballard and west Seattle.

**CORPORATE HISTORY**

● 1970: Boeing's decision to lay off 655,000 workers over a two-year period precipitates a recession.
● 1971: Starbucks opens in Pike Place Market, launching the nation's specialty coffee craze.
● 1975: Bill Gates and Paul Allen start Microsoft.
● 2000: The US Justice Department anti-trust rulings ordered the breakup of Microsoft. Microsoft appealed.
● 2001: Boeing moves its HQ to Chicago. The Seattle area reels from dot.com collapse.

# Time to Shop

*Below: Glasshouse Studio*
*Below right: Pike Place Public Market*

Greater Downtown has been a shopping destination since the Alaska Gold Rush, when the city became the chief outfitting post for prospectors heading north. One lucky miner

returned with a small nest egg to start a retail shoe business that has since grown into Seattle's most cherished department store—Nordstrom's (► 73), renowned for its customer service.

(► 73)

### SEATTLE'S SALES TAX

Don't be surprised at the 8 percent sales tax added to your purchases. Many locals believe this tax places an unfair burden on poor people and favor, instead, a state income tax (Washington has none). In this economic climate, however, it's unlikely that voters would approve a totally new levy. For better or worse, the sales tax is probably here to stay.

For small gifts, start at Pike Place Market, where farmers and artisans set up their stalls before 9am. The tables displaying fresh flower bouquets often carry dried arrangements that make excellent gifts. In the crafts area you'll find wood and metal items, as well as pottery, jewelry, textiles and regional food items like preserves, dried cherries and smoked fish. Don't miss the free samples.

Washington wines, having garnered top awards at international tastings, are another special purchase. Grapes are grown east of Washington's Cascade Range at the same latitude as the wine-making provinces of France—Pike Market Cellars offers a good selection. You can sample the local wines at one of the tasting rooms close to the city—try Chateau St. Michelle, 15 miles northeast

of downtown in Woodinville, Washington states oldest winery (founded in 1934). To recreate Northwest cuisine at home, stop at Post Alley for a look at local cookbooks penned by world-class

*Below and left: Pike Place Market*

### FINE ART

Seattle's fine arts galleries and crafts shops are concentrated in downtown malls, around the Seattle Art Museum and in Pioneer Square. Many feature Native American art of the Northwest Coast. You will find not only antiques—Native American baskets, jewelry, early Edward Curtis photographs, ceremonial masks and wood carvings—but also striking contemporary prints and carvings created by Native American artists working today. Fine woodworking is also on display at the cooperative Northwest Gallery of Fine Woodworking, a furniture showroom. Here you can view exceptional craftsmanship and one-of-a-kind designs, and commission a piece by the artist of your choice.

Seattle chefs like Tom Douglas. Cookbooks are also available at the Made in Washington (► 77) shop, which carries only items that are made, produced or grown in the state. Seattle's glass-blowers, working in the tradition of the Pilchuk School (► 75) exhibit and sell their brilliant wares in galleries and studios throughout the city. For the tacky and the bizarre, check out the tourist haunts along Seattle's waterfront and the funky shops in Fremont. For joke and novelty items, you can't beat Archie McPhee's.

Today, to find the greatest variety of stores in a compact area; head straight for downtown, the Pike Place Market and neighboring Belltown and Pioneer Square. Seattle reigns as a manufacturer and retailer of outdoor and recreational apparel. Outfitters are located both downtown and in the corridor between Eastlake and Westlake, where REI (► 74) resides. Visit downtown department stores and upscale malls like Westlake Center and Pacific Place—or check out Belltown designer boutiques along 1st and 2nd avenues.

# Out and About

Above: *Empress Hotel, Nictorial*; right: *Mt. Ranier*

## ORGANIZED SIGHTSEEING

Gray Line Tours (☎ 206/626–5208; www. graylineofseattle.com) offer city tours; evening tours on a double-decker bus; Tillicum Village boat trips for traditional salmon roast and Native American dancing; Boeing tours; day and

overnight trips to Mt. Rainier, the Olympic Peninsula, the San Juan Islands and Vancouver, Victoria, BC, and tours leave from the Washington State Convention Center. Seattle Tours (☎ 206/768–1234) offers tours of downtown 9.30am and 2pm, as well as day trips further afield. Viewpoints Architectural Walking Tours (☎ 206/667–9186; www. seattlearchitectural.org/essential/htm) runs tours from May to November. You can get a bird's-eye view with Seattle Seaplanes (☎ 206/329–9638 or 800/637–5533; www.seattleseaplanes.com) and Kenmore Air Seaplanes (☎ 425/486–1257 or 800/543–9595; www.kenmoreair.com).

## EXCURSIONS
### VICTORIA, BRITISH COLUMBIA
High-speed catamarans cruise Puget Sound and the Strait of Juan de Fuca, and sail into beautiful Victoria for a taste of merry England (with formal gardens, double-decker buses and shops selling tweeds and Irish linen). At the Royal British Columbia Museum you can view items made by Native Americans living on the Northwest Coast. Or you can meander through the Butchart Gardens or indulge yourself with tea in the imperial splendor of the Empress Hotel.

## MT. RAINIER

Mt. Rainier, one of a string of active volcanoes running south from the Canadian border to California, rises 14,410ft (4,392m) above sea level, and the upper 6,000ft (1,800m) are covered in snow year-round. On clear days, its

white dome, hovering over Seattle, has an appearance so awesome and so immediate that it's hard to believe it's 70 miles (113m) away. Small wonder that native peoples ascribed supernatural power to the mountain. For a closer view of the peak, drive to Crystal Mountain and take the chairlift to its summit. For information on hiking, stop at Longmire, then drive 11 miles (18km) to the Paradise Visitor Center, where many trails begin.

## HURRICANE RIDGE/OLYMPIC NATIONAL PARK

Take the ferry to Bainbridge Island (► 36). From there, take route 305 west to 3 north, then pick up route 104. Follow route 20 to Victorian Port Townsend, pausing for coffee before doubling back to US 101 west and Port Angeles. Turn south on Hurricane Ridge Road and drive the 17 winding miles (27km) to the Olympic National Park Visitor Center. Walk the 1.5-mile (2.5-km) trail to Hurricane Hill, watching for marmot and deer. To see the Elwha River rainforest, return to Port Angeles, continuing west on route 101 the short distance to Olympic Hot Springs Road. Feast your eyes on the lush vegetation and watch for elk. From here, retrace the route to Seattle, and if time permits, walk Dungeness Spit.

### INFORMATION

### MT. RAINIER
**Distance** 90 miles (145km) southeast of Seattle
**Journey Time** 3 hours by road
**Route** I-5 south to Tacoma; east on route 512; south on route 7 and east on route 706 to the park entrance
**Bus Tours** Gray Line (► 20); Scenic Bound Tours ☎ 206/433–6907; Mt. Rainier Tours ☎ 206/768–1234
**Mt. Rainier National Park** ☎ 360/569–2211; www.mount.rainier.national-park.com
**Paradise Visitor Center** ☎ 360/589–2275

### INFORMATION

### HURRICANE RIDGE/ OLYMPIC NATIONAL PARK
**Distance** 190-mile (305-km) round trip
**Journey Time** 2.5 hours by road to Port Townsend (a long day trip)
**Olympic National Park Visitor Center** ☎ 360/452–0330; www.olympic.national-park.com
🚩 On your return journey, stop at Fat Smitty's located on Discovery Bay, for a burger, or feast on Dungeness crab at Three Crabs on US 101.

# Walks

## THE SIGHTS

- Freeway Park (➤ 52)
- Rainier Square
- Blueprints: 100 Years of Seattle Architecture—free exhibit at the Museum of History and Industry (➤ 54)
- Fifth Avenue Theater (➤ 56)
- City Center (➤ 37)
- Westlake Center
- Westlake Park
- Pike Place Market (➤ 35)

*Right:* Freeway Park

## INFORMATION

**Distance** 1.5miles (2.4km)
**Time** 2 hours without stops
**Start point** ★ The Washington Convention Center, 8th and Pike
🚇 E6
🚌 7, 10, 43 on Pike
**End point** Harbor Steps, University Street between 1st Avenue and Western
🚇 F6
🚃 Waterfront streetcar

## CITY CENTER TO PIKE PLACE MARKET

Begin at the Seattle/King County Visitor Center on the galleria level of the Washington State Convention and Trade Center. Pick up a calendar of events and a discount coupon book; then walk to the central lobby, where you'll pass under an imposing carved doorway to board the escalator to Level 4. Exit through Freeway Park to the park's southwest corner. Descend the concrete stairs through the Canyon waterfall, designed to mask traffic noise from the freeway underneath. Leave the park at 6th and University, cross University, and climb the stairs to Union Square for a view of the city from the spacious plaza.

Double back to University, heading west to Rainier Square. Look at the Seattle architecture

exhibit, on Level 3, and exit on 5th across from the Fifth Avenue Theater and Eddie Bauer. Head north across Union, past the City Center, and cross Pike and Pine to the Westlake Center. The glass-walled Seattle's Best Coffee, opposite Westlake Park, is a good place for a java break. Head down Pine to 1st. Walk north one block to Stewart, the head left for half a block to Post Alley and right down the narrow way to Virginia. Stroll past Pike Place Fish. Continue south until you are facing Tenzing Momo Herbal Apothecary; then head down the stairs on your left, winding along an interior corridor past Pike Place Brewery until you come out at 1st and Union across from the Seattle Art Museum. One block south, at 1st Avenue and University, you'll reach Harbor Steps (➤ 56).

## Waterfront to Pioneer Square

Stroll down the Harbor Steps and amble south along the Waterfront to Yesler. Turn left and walk to the corner of 1st and Yesler, site of Pioneer Square's pergola. Cross to the east side of 1st and walk south, taking time to drift into shops along the way. Cross Washington, pass Grand Central Arcade, and continue across Main to the amazing and entirely unique Elliott Bay Bookstore. Then proceed along 1st to Jackson and go left one block to cobblestoned Occidental, then left again onto its pedestrian mall. Step into the shops and galleries along the way, and if possible, catch a glass-blowing demonstration at Glasshouse Art Glass.

At Main, visit the Klondike Gold Rush National Historic Park, just left of Occidental. The

Left: *Pioneer Square*

museum commemorates Seattle's role as an outfitting center for prospectors. As you exit, turn right and walk past Occidental Park, noting the totem poles, and continue to Waterfall Park, a serene oasis at 2nd Avenue. Walk right on 2nd one block to Jackson to see the lovely Rain Forest Gate. Catch any bus northbound on 2nd Avenue or walk southeast to Metro's International District bus station. Exit the bus station at University and drop into Benaroya Hall, home of the Seattle Symphony, to see the enormous chandeliers by Northwest glass artist Dale Chihuly. Now, walk to Washington Mutual's blue tower (► 56) at 3rd and Seneca. Finally walk uphill for one block to the elegant Four Seasons Olympic Hotel, where you can have drinks in the Terrace Room.

### THE SIGHTS

### INFORMATION

**Distance** 1.5 miles (2.4km)
**Time** 2 hours without stops
**Start** ★Harbor Steps, 1st Avenue and University Street
➕ F6
🚋 Waterfront streetcar
**End point**
 Four Seasons Olympic Hotel, 4th and University
➕ F6
🚌 Free bus zone

# Seattle by Night

Above: *Ferry crossing Elliott Bay at twilight*
Right: *Space Needle by night*

## CLUBS FOR ALL

The Seattle club scene breaks down by neighborhood. Belltown hangouts that once played grunge now feature hip-hop, while other downtown nightclubs cater to an older, more upscale crowd that enjoys salsa dancing or listening to jazz. Pioneer Square has both stylish clubs as well as taverns that draw young singles by offering a joint cover and live R&B music on weekends. For rootsy folk and acoustic music, head to Ballard, where the scene is more laid-back. Capitol Hill along Pike and Pine is the place to find the city's gay bars and dance clubs.

After-hours entertainment in Seattle runs the gamut from classical music to spectator sports, comedy to swing dance. The Seattle Opera, Pacific Northwest Ballet, the Seattle Symphony, and several theater companies are in residence between late fall and spring, when dark days and drizzle limit outdoor activities. In May and June, the city hosts the Seattle International Film Festival, the nation's largest, and at any given time during the rest of the year, a half-dozen local cinemas are showing foreign or independent films. Concert venues like the Paramount and Fifth Avenue book touring artists all the time, and local theater companies stagger their plays so that audiences can enjoy live theater in every month.

In summer, an evening of baseball is fun; when Mariners' action flags, take a minute to check out the view from Safeco Field's upper deck. Another pleasant option is a twilight ferry ride across Elliott Bay; time the trip to catch the sunset on the way out and the lit-up skyline as you return by nightfall. Summer days are long—perfect for an evening stroll while it's still light followed by drinks and dinner on the patio of a waterfront restaurant.

On a cold winter's evening, stop for a cocktail at a swanky hotel lounge, quench your thirst at a Belltown tavern, or see what's on tap at one of Seattle's excellent brewpubs. Afterwards, you might head to one of Seattle's many clubs (►panel) for live music, dancing, comedy or improvisational theater.

# SEATTLE's
## top 25 sights

The sights are shown on the maps on the inside front cover and inside back cover, numbered **1**–**25** from west to east across the city

# Discovery Park

## INFORMATION

**Discovery Park**

- Off map L2; Locator map A3
- 3801 W Government Way
- 206/386–4236
- Park daily dawn to dusk. Visitor Center daily 8.30–5 (except national holidays)
- 33
- Poor
- Free
- Nature walks and classes; children's playground

**Daybreak Star Art Center**

- 206/285–4425
- Mon–Fri 9–5, Sat 10–5, Sun noon–5
- Very good
- Salmon lunch/Artmart, Sat in Dec; Seafair Indian Pow-Wow Days, third weekend in July

*Detail of one of the artworks inside Daybreak Star*

**This park is the largest stand of wilderness in the city. Its meadows, forests, cliffs, marshes and shoreline provide habitat for many birds and animals.**

**Legacy of the military** The 520 forested acres (211ha) on Magnolia Bluff that is today's Discovery Park was a military base from the 1890s, but in 1970, the government turned it over to the city for use as a park. During the transfer, an alliance of local tribes decided to take the opportunity to regain ancestral land they felt was theirs, and 19 acres (8ha) were set aside for a Native American cultural center.

**Discover the trails** The park's great size means that there are miles of nature and bike trails to be explored. Test your fitness along the half-mile "parcours" (health path) through the woods. To the west, 2 miles (3km) of beach extend north and south from the West Point lighthouse (head south for sand, north for rocks). To get to the beach, pick up the loop trail at the north or south parking lot. The park's Visitor Center provides free 90-minute walks led by a naturalist, every Saturday at 2pm.

**Daybreak Star Art Center** The structure uses enormous cedar timbers to reflect the points of a star. Native art adorns the walls inside. The Center's Sacred Circle Gallery of American Indian Art is one of only four showcases dedicated to contemporary Native American work in the country.

## Alki Beach

**Alki beach is Seattle's birthplace. Today, its sandy shore and waterfront trail are as close as Seattle gets to resembling Southern California.**

**Beginnings** The Duwamish and Suquamish peoples were on hand to meet the schooner *Exact* when it sailed into Elliott Bay on 13 November 1851. The ship anchored off Alki Point and Arthur Denny and his party of 23 paddled their skiff ashore. The locals proved friendly and the Denny party decided to stay. They set about building four log cabins, wistfully naming their new home New York–Alki, "Alki" being a word in the Chinook language for "someday," an indication of Denny's ambitions. The following year, after surviving fierce winter storms, the settlers decided to move across Elliott Bay to the more sheltered, deepwater harbor that is today's Pioneer Square.

**Beach life** The beach itself is the main attraction today. There are great views, fine sand, a paved trail and boat and bike rentals. There's food and drink, too—try Pegasus (for pizza) and the Alki Bakery (for cookies and other sweets). You can walk, bike, or skate the 2.5 miles (4km) from Alki Beach to Duwamish Head. If you wish, continue south along the water to lovely Lincoln Park where an outdoor saltwater pool and waterslide invite a refreshing dip (► 53).

### INFORMATION

🔳 Off map L2;
Locator map A4
✉️ 3201 Alki Avenue SW
(Alki Point Light Station)
🕐 Lighthouse Sat–Sun
noon–4 and some
holidays. Coast Guard
officer on duty May–Aug
to answer questions
🚌 37 from 2nd Avenue (no
night or weekend
service); 56 southbound
on 1st Avenue
♿ Wheelchair access along
paved trail
↔️ Lincoln Park (► 53)
❓ Bike, inline skate and
boat rentals (► 58–59);
driftwood fires
permitted on beach

*The Alki Point Light Station looks across Puget Sound*

27

# The Hiram M. Chittenden Locks

*Above: The turbulent waters of the Chittenden Locks*

**Legions of boat owners pass through these locks when taking their boats from freshwater into Puget Sound. Alongside, salmon struggle to climb a fish ladder on the miraculous return to their spawning grounds.**

**A dream comes true** The 1917 opening of the Ballard Locks and Lake Washington Ship Canal was the fulfillment of a 60-year-old pioneer dream to build a channel that would link Lake Washington and Puget Sound. Primitive construction attempts were made in the 1880s, but it wasn't until Major Hiram M. Chittenden, regional director of the Army Corps of Engineers, won Congressional approval in 1910, that work began in earnest. Over the next six years, workers excavated and moved thousands of tons of earth with giant steam shovels. The locks are operated from a control tower that regulates the spillway gates and flashes directions to boats. Displays in the nearby Visitor Center explain the history and construction of the locks and ship canal. One-hour guided tours leave from the center on weekends at 2pm.

**Watch the fish** A fish ladder, built into the locks, allows salmon and steelhead to move upstream from the sea to their spawning grounds. By sensing "attraction water" at the fish ladder's entrance, the fish find the narrow channel and begin the long journey to the very freshwater spot where they began life. Here, they lay their eggs and die.

**Botanical Gardens** Nearby, you can also explore the 7-acre (3-ha) Carl S. English Jr. Botanical Gardens, which are planted with more than 500 species from around the world.

## Fishermen's Terminal

**Fishermen's Terminal is a great place to soak up the comings and goings of a large fleet. Here, fishermen mend their nets and prepare to head north or return, tie up and unload their catch.**

**Early days** Fish have been an important local resource since Seattle's early days, when the Shilshoh people from Salmon Bay first shared their bountiful harvest with other local tribes. With white settlement, fishing became an important local industry. In the early 1900s, a growing demand for salmon prompted the industry to lure new fishermen to the area—especially Scandinavian, Greek and Slavic immigrants—many of whose descendants still work in the fishing trade. In 1913, the Port of Seattle designated Fishermen's Terminal on Salmon Bay as home base for the North Pacific fishing fleet. Today Washington fishers harvest 50 percent of all fish and other seafood caught in the United States.

**Fishermen's Memorial** Dominating the terminal's central plaza, a 30-ft (9-m) high column commemorates those Northwest fishermen who lost their lives at sea. Their names are inscribed at the memorial sculpture's base and serve to remind us that fishing was—and remains— extremely dangerous work and that the sea can be cruelly unforgiving.

### DID YOU KNOW?

- More than 600 commercial fishing boats are based at the terminal, many bound for Alaska
  - Gillnetters, purse seiners and trawlers use nets; longliners and trollers use lines
  - Trollers have a midship pole, hung at a 45-degree angle, to which baited lines are secured

### INFORMATION

- ✚ Off map L2; Locator map A3
- ✉ 3919 18th Avenue Wat, Salmon Bay
- ☎ 206/728–3395
- ⏰ 24 hours
- 🚌 15 or 18 from 1st Avenue (Exit south of Ballard Bridge) or 33 from 4th Avenue
- ♿ Very good
- 🎟 Free
- 🔗 Discovery Park (▶ 26)
- ❓ Chinooks Restaurant, a wild fish market, gallery, grocery and marine shops

*The Fishermen's Memorial is topped by a bronze sculpture of a halibut fisherman*

29

## Woodland Park Zoo

**Woodland Park Zoo has won international recognition for its progressive design and is a highly respected leader in wildlife conservation. The animals move freely in settings that resemble their natural habitats.**

**Running free (almost)** Most animals roam freely in their approximated "bioclimatic zones." Four exhibits—African Savanna, Tropical Rain Forest, Northern Trail (Alaska) and Elephant Forest—have won prestigious awards and introduced zoo visitors not only to the animals, but also to corresponding plant species and ecosystems. The newest permanent exhibits include a southern African floodplain-riverbank habitat where rare African wildhogs live, the amazing replica of an African village, an exhibit of the rare Dragons of Komodo, the world's largest lizards, and the Trail of Vines, which showcases macaques, tapirs, pythons and orang-utans in a setting representing the forests of western India and northern Borneo.

**Zoo newcomers** The newest arrivals, a pair of Siberian tiger cubs born late in 2002, were introduced to the public in the summer of 2003. Other relative newcomers that continue to delight include Hansa, the Asian elephant calf born on-site, and Naku, a western lowland gorilla whose name means "queen of the forest."

*Gorilla mother and child at Woodland Park Zoo*

## Pacific Science Center

**As you approach the Pacific Science Center, you enter another world. Soaring gothic arches and an inner courtyard of reflecting pools, platforms and footbridges indicate you are in for something special.**

**Sputnik's legacy** In 1962, the American scientific community was still smarting from the Soviet Union's unexpected launch of the Sputnik spacecraft. Determined to restore confidence in American science and technology, US officials pulled out all the stops when they built the US Science Pavilion for the Seattle World's Fair. The building reopened after the fair ended as the Pacific Science Center.

**Science made easy** A visit to the Pacific Science Center can happily fill half a day. The interactive exhibits bring scientific principles to life and make learning fun. In an outdoor exhibit, Water Works, you can manoeuvre a water cannon to activate whirligigs or attempt to move a 2-ton ball suspended on water. Nearby, children can ride a high-rail bike for a bird's-eye view of proceedings. The Body Works exhibition lets you measure your stress level, grip strength and mental concentration, or see what your face looks like with two left sides. In the Tech Zone's Virtual Basketball installation, you stand against a backdrop, put on a virtual reality glove, and by moving an arm, transport yourself to a computer screen where you can go one-on-one against an on-screen opponent. Or, challenge a robot to a game of tic-tac-toe. The Science Playground and Brain Game areas use giant levers, spinning rooms and baseball batting cages to teach the principles of physics. Small children like blowing giant bubbles and climbing the rocket in the Kids' Zone. Next door is the IMAX 3-D Theater.

### DID YOU KNOW?

- Designed by Minoru Yamasaki
- Built as the US Science Pavilion for the 1962 World's Fair
- The first museum in the United States to be founded as a science and technology center

### INFORMATION

- D2; Locator map D2
- 200 2nd Avenue N (Seattle Center)
- 206/443-2001; www.pacsci.org
- Mon–Fri 10–5, Sat–Sun 10–6
- Fountains Café
- 1, 2, 3, 4, 13, 16, 24, 33
- Monorail
- Very good
- Moderate; half-price with CityPass (seniors free on Wed)
- Space Needle (▶ 32), Experience Music Project (▶ 33), Monorail (▶ 37)
- Two IMAX 3-D theaters (206/443–IMAX); Laser Theater presents family matinees and evening rock shows (206/443–2850)

*Above: Hands-on fun at the Water Works exhibit* 31

# Space Needle

## DID YOU KNOW?

- The Space Needle sways about 1in (3cm) for every 10mph (16kph) of wind
- The Needle experienced an earthquake of 6.8 on the Richter scale (in 2001), and is equipped to withstand jolts up to 9.2

## INFORMATION

- D3; Locator map D2
- Seattle Center
- 206/905–2100 or 800/937–9582
- Observation Deck Sun–Thu 9am–11pm, Fri–Sat 9am–midnight
- Sky City Restaurant
- 3, 4, 16
- Monorail
- Wheelchair access
- Expensive; half-price with CityPass; free with dinner at restaurant
- Pacific Science Center (► 31), Experience Music Project (► 33), Monorail (► 37)

**The Space Needle's height and futuristic design have made it Seattle's most well-known landmark. The view from the observation deck is stunning on a clear day.**

**The city's symbol** The 605-ft (184-m) Space Needle was built in 1962 for Seattle's futuristic World's Fair. Rising 200ft (61m) above Seattle's highest hill, the structure is visible over a wide area. The steel structure weighs 3,700 tons and is anchored into the foundation with 72 huge bolts, each 32ft (10m) long by 4in (10cm) in diameter. The structure is designed to withstand winds up to 150mph (242kph). If you ride in the glass-walled elevator to the top during a snowstorm, it appears to be snowing upward.

**Observation deck** Each year, more than a million visitors ride one of the three glass elevators to the observation deck at the 520ft (159m) level. Informative displays point out more than 60 sites around the area and recount Space Needle facts and trivia. Free high-resolution telescopes allow you to

zoom in on objects for a closer view. A reservation at the SkyCity Restaurant on the 500th level gets you to the observation deck free of charge. The restaurant rotates one complete turn every 47 minutes, giving you a wonderful 360-degree panorama view during the course of your meal.

*A view of Seattle from the Needle's observation deck*

# Experience Music Project (EMP)

**Seattle has entered the 21st century with a dazzling rock 'n' roll museum and musical gathering place. This temple to American music is unrivaled in both scale and daring.**

**Gift to the city** Co-founder of Microsoft, Paul Allen idolized Seattle-born Jimi Hendrix and imagined a space to exhibit his personal collection of Hendrix memorabilia. Over time, the vision expanded beyond Hendrix: The museum would explore all of American popular music through interactive and interpretive exhibits.

**The design** Allen hired celebrated architect Frank O. Gehry to create a structure that would reflect the rebelliousness that characterizes rock 'n' roll. To jumpstart his design, Gehry cut up and rearranged several brightly-colored electric guitars. This gave birth to EMP's bold colors, sweeping curves and reflective metal surface.

**Inside** The 85-ft (26-m) "Sky Church" features music film and video by day and live bands at night. Trace the development of the electric guitar or view artifacts of Seattle "Grunge," jam on real instruments in the Sound Lab or record your own voice. On the Artist's Journey, travel the world of rock 'n' roll through image, sound, lighting, special effects and motion technology.

## DID YOU KNOW?

- Jazz musician Les Paul pioneered electric guitar technology in Seattle by using a solid body. The Gibson company adopted the design and use it to this day
- Jimi Hendrix was born in Seattle in 1942. In the late 1960s he revolutionized electric guitar playing a radical fusion of jazz, rock, soul and blues

## INFORMATION

- ✚ D3; Locator map D2
- ✉ Seattle Center
- ☎ 206/367–5483 or 877/EMPLIVE; www.emplive.com
- 🕐 Sun–Thu 10–6, Fri–Sat 9–9; shorter hours in winter
- 🚌 3, 4, 16
- ↔ Pacific Science Center (▶ 31), Space Needle (▶ 33), Monorail (▶ 37)
- ♿ Good
- 💲 Expensive

*Jimi Hendrix, Seattle native and guitar hero*

# The Waterfront & Aquarium

**The aquarium**
- Children's touch tank
- Underwater dome room
- Coral reef exhibit

**The waterfront**
- Bell Street complex restaurants and marina
- Waterfront trolley
- Odyssey Maritime Discovery Center
- Russian submarine

## INFORMATION

**The aquarium**
- ➕ F5; Locator map E3
- ✉ Pier 59: 1483 Alaskan Way at Pike Street
- ☎ 206/386–4320; www.seattleaquarium.org
- 🕐 Daily 10–7, Jun–Aug; daily 10–5, rest of year
- 🍴 Steamers Seafood Cafe
- 🚋 Waterfront streetcar (Pike Street station)
- ♿ Very good
- 🎟 Moderate; half-price with CityPass

**The waterfront**
- ✉ Alaskan Way between Broad (pier 70) and Main (pier 48)
- 🚋 33; waterfront streetcar

**Seattle's history and economic growth have been closely tied to the waterfront since 1853, when Henry Yesler built the first sawmill at the foot of the hill that bears his name.**

**Starting out** When pioneers settled along Elliott Bay's eastern shores in 1852, the only flat land suitable for building was a narrow strip along the water, where 1st Avenue runs today. A century later, Seattle's landscape had changed dramatically, after a large expanse of Elliott Bay was reclaimed. Maritime industrial activity had moved south to pier 46 and below, and the downtown waterfront was ripe for new beginnings.

**Seattle Aquarium** This is *the* place to acquaint yourself with Northwest marine life. In the underwater dome room you can watch Puget Sound's "underworld" pass before your eyes. The Aquarium's newest exhibit features "leafy sea dragons"—foot-long seahorses with what look to be greenish or golden branches. Other highlights include the exceptional Pacific coral reef exhibit and, for children who enjoy touching critters, the hands-on Discovery Lab.

**Watery hub** Import stores, restaurants and excursion boats dot the waterfront. The Odyssey Maritime Discovery Center at pier 66 (Bell Street Complex) features interactive exhibits that illuminate the workings of a large port. At pier 48, those who lived through the Cold War will be interested in touring the *Cobra*, a combat Russian submarine of the Soviet Navy that plied the waters on secret missions for 20 years. A picturesque trolley picks up passengers and drops them off along the waterfront, then loops north to Pioneer Square and the International District.

*Above: The aquarium's underwater dome*

## Pike Place Market

**To many residents, Pike Place Market is Seattle's heart and soul. Here, people of every background converge, from city professionals and farmers to hippie craftsmen and tourists.**

**Farmers' market** Pike Place Market was founded in 1907 so that farmers could sell directly to the consumer and eliminate the middleman. It was an immediate success, and grew quickly until World War II precipitated a decline. Threatened by demolition in the 1960s, it's now protected as an Historic District.

**Feast for the senses** The three-block area stretching between Pike and Virginia has flowerstalls, fishsellers, produce displays, tea shops, bakeries, herbal apothecaries, magic stores and much more. Street musicians play Peruvian panpipes or sing the blues, and the fragrance of flowers and fresh bread fills the air. This is old Seattle frozen in time.

**Exploring the market** Pick up a map from the information booth (1st Avenue and Pike Street, near the big clock) and head out from the sculpture of Rachel the pig. Watch out for the flying fish (at Pike Place Fish), stop to admire the artfully arranged produce and flower displays and make a sweep around the crafts area, where superb handmade items are sold.

### HIGHLIGHTS

**Market Arcade**
- Stores: Read All About It (for newspapers), DiLaurenti's Grocery and Deli, Market Spice Teas, Tenzing Momo
- Restaurants: Athenian Inn, Sound View Café, Place Pigalle, Maximiliens

**Sanitary Market Building/Post Alley**
- Stores: Jack's Fish Spot, Milagros, Made in Washington

### INFORMATION

- F5; Locator map E3
- 1st Avenue between Stewart and Union
- 206/682-7453
- Mon–Sat 9–6, Sun 11–5. Closed some national holidays
- Rt. 10 on Pine and 1st–4th Avenue (free ride zone); waterfront streetcar
- Poor
- Market Theater Fri–Sun nights: www.unexpected-productions.org
- Seattle Aquarium (➤ 34), Seattle Art Museum (➤ 38), Pioneer Square (➤ 41)

*Pike Place Fish Co. is admired for its range of seafood*

35

# Ferry to Bainbridge Island

*The city drops away as the ferry heads to Bainbridge*

**There's nothing more delightful than catching a Washington State ferry to Bainbridge Island. Standing at the stern as the boat pulls away, you can see the entire Seattle skyline unfold.**

**The ferry** It takes just 35 minutes to get to Bainbridge Island from the downtown waterfront. En route, you'll see an amazing panorama: The Seattle cityscape and Mt. Rainier to the east, and Bainbridge Island and the snow-capped Olympic Range to the west.

**Touring on foot** Once you disembark at the Bainbridge ferry dock, walk the short distance to the town of Winslow, visit the charming boutiques, browse at Eagle Harbor Books, stop for lunch at Café Nola (▶ 70), or order treats from the Bainbridge Bakery. If it's Saturday, catch the market on the Winslow green, or, Wednesday to Sunday, visit Bainbridge's Island Winery for tasting. If you're synchronizing your return with the sunset, you could linger at the Harbour Public House (▶ 84).

**Touring by car or bike** If you have wheels, visit Bloedel Reserve and walk the exquisite

trails (call in advance for reservations). Continuing across Agate Pass Bridge on to the Kitsap Peninsula, you enter Port Madison Indian Reservation and the town of Suquamish, where leader Chief Sealth is buried. A museum shows the tribe's history.

## Monorail to Seattle Center

**Riding the Monorail to Seattle Center is like being in an old sci-fi movie. You buzz the city like a giant insect and sweep past Experience Music Project before alighting at the Center House.**

**World's Fair leftovers** The Seattle Center district, like the monorail, is the legacy of the 1962 World's Fair. Once a Native American ceremonial ground, and later host to traveling circuses, the 74-acre (30-ha) site didn't assume its present form until the fair. The monorail has now run continuously longer than any other monorail in the world.

**Museum city** Every day, this elevated train carries up to 7,000 passengers between Westlake Center, Seattle's retail core and Seattle Center, its entertainment hub. There, you can go on amusement park rides, take a trip in the Space Needle's glass elevator (▶ 32) or visit museums and galleries, including the Children's Museum (▶ 62), Experience Music Project (▶ 33), several craft galleries and the Pacific Science Center (▶ 31). Seattle Center is also home to opera, ballet, excellent theater companies (▶ 80) and several professional sports teams. Also, Seattle's major festivals take place on the center grounds. Stop in the Center House for something to eat or try one of the restaurants close by.

**Easy walking** Stroll through the delightful Sculpture Garden and the adjacent Peace Garden southwest of the Needle, or enjoy a picnic on the grass by the International Fountain.

### INFORMATION

**Monorail to Seattle Center**

➕ E6; Locator map E3

✉ Downtown station 3rd floor, Westlake Center; Seattle Center Station adjacent to EMP

☎ Seattle Center 206/684–7200 or 206/684–8582 (recorded event line); www.seattlecenter.com

🕐 Monorail daily every 10 minutes. Seattle Center grounds Mon–Fri 7.30–11pm, Sat–Sun 9–11pm

🍴 Seattle Center House; closed Thanksgiving, Christmas and New Year

🚌 3, 4, 16

🎟 Free to Center grounds

*The monorail station at Westlake Center*

# Seattle Art Museum

## HIGHLIGHTS

- Jonathan Borofsky's sculpture *Hammering Man*
- Indigenous art of Africa, Oceania, and the Americas
- The Katherine White collection of African sculpture
- Northwest Coast collection

## INFORMATION

- F5; Locator map E3
- 100 University Street
- 206/654–3100
- Tue–Sun 10–5 (Thu till 9). Closed Mon except holiday Mondays. Closed Thanksgiving, Christmas and New Year
- Museum Café
- Through tunnel or along 1st, 2nd or 3rd (free-ride zone)
- Very good
- Moderate; half-price with CityPass. Admission ticket good for both downtown museum and Asian Art Museum in Volunteer Park. Free on first Thu of month; free for those over 62, first Fridays
- "Thursday After Hours" features poetry and music

**Some people love it; some can do without it. No one, however, fails to notice the imposing Seattle Art Museum or the 48-ft (15-m) black metal sculpture that dominates its entrance.**

**Another world** The pink granite arcaded structure of the Seattle Art Museum (SAM), opened in 1991, steps up the hill between 1st and 2nd Avenues. To reach the galleries, you ascend a grand staircase, walking the gauntlet between monumental paired rams, guardian figures and sacred camels from the Ming dynasty.

**Dazzling collections** SAM's permanent collections range from the indigenous art of Africa, Oceania and the Americas to modern US paintings and sculpture. Other galleries feature European painting and sculpture from the Medieval period through the 19th century. The Katherine White collection of African sculpture, masks, textiles and decorative arts is beautifully displayed, while a Northwest Coast collection features both small items, such as baskets and dream catchers, as well as much larger pieces, including four full-scale carved Kwakiutl houseposts. In other galleries, the museum presents traveling exhibitions and launches major shows of its own. Recent exhibitions have featured ancient Chinese art from Sichuan, Annie Liebovitz photographs and major retrospective shows of Mexican artist Frida Kahlo and African-American artist Jacob Lawrence.

*Hammering Man* Of the 48-ft (15-m) sculpture out front sculptor Jonathan Borofsky has said: "I want this work to appeal to all people of Seattle—not just artists, but families young and old. At its heart, society reveres the worker. The *Hammering Man* is the worker in all of us."

## Lake Union

**In a neighborhood shared by tugboats and research ships, ducks and racoons, Lake Union's houseboaters swop dry land and backyards for a vibrant lifestyle on this bustling lake.**

**Floating world** The houseboat life started over a century ago on Lake Union. A sawmill that opened on the lake in 1881 attracted a community of loggers and their hangers-on. Many of these woodsmen built themselves makeshift shelters by tying felled logs together and erecting tarpaper shacks on top. Before long, thousands of shacks floated on the waterways. These "floating homes," Seattle's earliest houseboats, were a far cry from the gentrified versions made familiar by the film *Sleepless in Seattle*.

**Boats and stores** Today Lake Union is a lively mix of marine activity, houseboat living and expensive dining and shopping. Start your visit with a stroll, passing the 468-ton schooner *Wawona*, and the Center for Wooden Boats on the south end to get right into the saltwater spirit. Then, for a true Lake Union experience, go out on the lake. You can rent sailboats, skiffs or kayaks, and explore on your own (▶ 59), or sign on with a tour (▶ 20). Back ashore, be sure to have a meal at one of the numerous good restaurants on Chandler's Cove.

### DID YOU KNOW?

- Seattle has more houseboats than anywhere east of Asia, and most are on Lake Union
- Lake Union took its name from a pioneer's speech in which he dreamed that one day, a lake would form "the union" between Puget Sound and Lake Washington
- Visitors who want to experience lakefront living can stay in a "bunk and breakfast" anchored in the lake
- Gasworks Park on the north side offers great views of downtown and is the city's premier kite-flying spot

### INFORMATION

- Locator map E1
- 70, 71, 72, 73 on Fairview/Eastlake
- Argosy Lake tours and "Discover Houseboating" tours (▶ 20), Seattle Seaplanes and Kenmore Air (▶ 20), Kayak, rowboat and sailboat rentals (▶ 59)

*A "street" of houseboat homes on Lake Union*

# Downtown

## INFORMATION

**Downtown Commercial Center**

- Locator map E3
- Between 3rd and 7th Avenues, and Stewart and University Street
- Through bus tunnel and on Pike, Pine, 3rd, 4th (free-ride zone)
- Monorail, Westlake Center
- None
- Pike Place Market (➤ 35), Seattle Art Museum (➤ 38), Pioneer Square (➤ 41), Belltown (➤ 57), Freeway Park (➤ 52)

**These days, downtown is jumping. Old buildings have resurfaced as theaters, while new stores, restaurants and hotels continue to spring up.**

**Vertical Seattle** The Seattle skyline began to change in the 1960's and by the mid-1980's more than two dozen new skyscrapers had dramatically altered the cityscape. Seattle's tallest building, the 76-story Columbia Seafirst Center, is located at 4th Avenue and Cherry, between Seattle's commercial core and Pioneer Square.

**Getting your bearings** The phrase "Downtown Seattle" is a rather ambiguous term that usually refers to a large area encompassing the Denny Regrade (Belltown), Pike Place Market, Pioneer Square and the International District. Seattle's retail core, however, is concentrated roughly in the center between University and Stewart, and between 3rd and 7th Avenues. Most stores, restaurants, hotels and travel offices are clustered in and around Westlake Center, City Center, Rainier Square and Union Square.

**Shopping** Triangular Westlake Park, with its public art and curtain of water, is a popular gathering place, especially when steel bands are jamming. Across the square, Westlake Center lures shoppers with its food court and specialty stores. South of Westlake, chain stores like Abercrombie & Fitch, Niketown, FAO Schwartz, and Banana Republic have moved in, while a state-of-the-art video arcade and two multiplex cinemas offer contemporary entertainment nearby. Also check out City Center's exclusive stores, the Palomino Bistro (at 5th Avenue and Pike), and The Sharper Image, an emporium devoted to high-tech gadgets. At 5th and Union, you'll pass Eddie Bauer (➤ 72), America's first outdoor retailer.

## Pioneer Square

**Constructed after the Great Seattle Fire, Pioneer Square's brick buildings retain an architectural integrity you won't find elsewhere in the city.**

**From the ashes** In 1852, Seattle's pioneers moved across Elliott Bay and built the first permanent settlement in what is now Pioneer Square. The area burned to the ground in 1889, but was quickly rebuilt. When gold was discovered in the Yukon, prospectors converged on Pioneer Square to board ships to Alaska, and the area became the primary outfitting post for miners.

**Moving through the square** Pioneer Square's most notable landmarks include Smith Tower (▶ 56) and the lovely glass-and-iron pergola at 1st and Yesler (repaired in 2001). Interesting stores line 1st Avenue south of Yesler. Walk through the lovely Grand Central Arcade, which opens onto Occidental Park and cross Main Street, taking time to visit the Klondike Gold Rush National Historic Park. Take a short detour to enchanting Waterfall Park at 2nd and South Main; then backtrack to the bricked pedestrian walkway, and amble along Occidental Place, taking time to explore the cluster of art galleries that extend around the corner to 1st and South Jackson. Browse at Elliott Bay Book Company; then dine at one of the area's excellent restaurants, catch some live music, or head for laughs at the Comedy Underground.

### HIGHLIGHTS

- The pergola at 1st and Yesler
- Smith Tower
- Occidental Park and totem poles
- Klondike Gold Rush National Historic Park
- Waterfall Park
- The Elliott Bay Book Company bookstore

### INFORMATION

**Pioneer Square**
- ✚ G6; Locator map E4
- ✉ Yesler to King and 2nd Avenue to Elliott Bay; Visitor Information booth in Occidental Mall in summer

**Klondike Gold Rush National Historic Park**
- ✉ 117 S Main
- ☎ 206/553–7220
- 🕐 Daily 9–5
- 🚌 1st and 2nd Avenues (free-ride zone) and in bus tunnel (Pioneer Square Station). Waterfront trolley stop
- ♿ Wheelchair access
- 🆓 Free
- 🔄 Waterfront (▶ 34), Pike Place Market (▶ 35), Seattle Art Museum (▶ 38), International District (▶ 43), Harbor Steps (▶ 56)

*Nineteenth-century red-brick elegance at Pioneer Square*

41

# REI (Recreational Equipment Inc.)

**The popularity of Recreational Equipment Inc., Seattle's premier retailer of outdoor wear and equipment, is legendary. The annual garage sale draws hordes of devotees who gather like pilgrims at a holy shrine.**

**It began with an ice axe** REI had humble origins in the 1930s. It was founded by Seattle climbers Lloyd and Mary Anderson, when Lloyd's search for a high-quality, affordable ice axe ended in frustration—the one he wanted was not sold in the United States but could be ordered only from Europe. Anderson purchased one and soon his climbing buddies wanted their own. In 1938, 23 climbers banded together to form a member-owned co-operative in order to obtain mountaineering equipment unavailable in the United States.

**Try it out** REI's flagship store is *the* place to try before you buy. Under staff guidance, you can, for example, don a harness and scale the store's free-standing 65-ft (20-m) high indoor pinnacle. There is a "hiking trail," where you can test the toughness of boots; a trail designed for mountain-bike test rides; and test stations for camp stoves and water filtration systems. REI also carries a large selection of outdoor apparel and books.

*Test the gear on the store's climbing pinnacle*

# The International District

**Bordered by the sparkling Union Station office park and two sports stadiums, Seattle's International District is home to the city's Chinese, Japanese, Filipino, Southeast Asian, Korean and other Asian communities.**

**Multicultural mix** The first Asian people to arrive in Seattle were Chinese men, who moved north from California to build the railways. Anti-Chinese riots broke out in the 1880s and many Chinese were deported, only to return after 1889 to help rebuild the charred settlement. The Japanese arrived next, many establishing small farms and selling their goods at Pike Place Market. The Filipinos, the third group to arrive, now constitute Seattle's largest Asian community.

**The neighborhood** Smaller and more modest than San Francisco's Chinatown, the International District caters primarily to those who live and work in the neighborhood. Start your exploration at the Wing Luke Asian Museum to get a sense of Seattle's rich Asian and Pacific Island heritage. Permanent exhibits include "One Song, Many Voices," which profiles the Asian and Pacific Islander immigration to this region, and "Camp Harmony D-4-44," a replica of the Japanese internment camp. Before leaving the museum pick up a map of the neighborhood. Make sure to include Hing Hay Park and Uwajimaya, the largest Asian emporium in the Northwest.

**Eat city** The district has many excellent Asian restaurants. Good bets include House of Hong for dim sum; Shanghai Garden for a Chinese lunch; or Yoshinobu for Japanese fare. For Vietnamese food, head up to 12th and Jackson ("Little Saigon") and try Saigon Bistro, or for Malaysian cuisine, check out Malay Satay at 12th and Main.

## HIGHLIGHTS

- The many Asian restaurants
- Wing Luke Museum
- Hing Hay Park, with its ornate pavilion and dragon mural
- Uwajimaya, a large Asian emporium

## INFORMATION

**The International District**
- E4, F4; Locator map F4
- Between S Main and Lane Street and 5th and 8th Avenues S; "Little Saigon" 12th S and Jackson.

**Wing Luke Asian Museum**
- 407 7th Avenue S
- 206/623-5124; www.wingluke.org
- Tue–Fri 11–4.30, Sat–Sun noon–4
- 1, 7 and 14 to Maynard and Jackson, 36 and bus tunnel (International District Station). Waterfront trolley to Jackson Street Station
- Wheelchair access for museum only
- Inexpensive
- Pioneer Square (➤ 41)
- Chinese New Year celebration in February

43

## Volunteer Park

### DID YOU KNOW?

- The park began to assume its present form in 1904
- The water tower is 75ft (23m) high
- The Seattle Asian Art Museum was collector Richard Fuller's gift to Seattle in 1932

### INFORMATION

**Volunteer Park**

- C4, C5; Locator map B3
- Between E Galer and E Prospect and 15th and 11th Avenues
- Park daily dawn to dusk. Conservatory daily 10–7, summer; 10–4, rest of year
- Free
- 10, 7
- Poor

**Seattle Asian Art Museum**

- 1400 E Prospect
- 206/654–3100; www.seattleartmuseum.org
- Tue–Sun 10–5 (Thu till 9), Memorial Day–Labor Day; Wed–Sun 10–5 (Thu till 9), rest of year; open holiday Mondays
- Fair
- Moderate; free first Thu and Sat of month, and first Fri for seniors. Free with SAAM admission

**Volunteer Park offers more than a lush green space. There's a conservatory, a water tower to climb for views and Seattle's Asian Art Museum.**

**Seattle Asian Art Museum (SAAM)** Carl Gould's art-deco building once housed the entire Seattle Art Museum (SAM) collection (➤ 38). In 1991 the Seattle Art Museum moved into a new downtown building, leaving the Volunteer Park facility to focus exclusively on Asian art. In addition to frequent special exhibitions of art and artifacts from across Asia, SAAM's Volunteer Park galleries showcase the museum's permanent collection numbering over 7,000 objects from China, Japan, Korea, India and Southeast Asia. The extensive Chinese collection, dating from the Neolithic period through the 19th century, includes ancient burial ceramics, ritual bronzes, snuff bottles and the wonderful *Monk Caught at the Moment of Enlightenment*. Japanese galleries feature Buddhist sculpture, metalwork, textiles, ink painting and calligraphy, including a portion of an early 17th-century "deer scroll," considered a Japanese national treasure. SAAM also offers Sunday afternoon concerts and dance programs, often in the central Garden Court.

**Outside the museum** Volunteer Park was named during the Spanish-American War of 1898 to honor those who had served as soldiers. Climb the water tower for a splendid 360-degree view, or stroll through the graceful Conservatory, where thousands of plants in five separate rooms simulate botanical environments from around the world. In winter, there's nothing like stepping into the tropics room, filled with giant ferns, palm sand orchids. Just north of the park boundaries at Lake View Cemetery (➤ 60), you can pay tribute at the graves of actor and martial arts legend Bruce Lee and his son, Brandon.

## Museum of Flight

**This stunning building is quite simply the finest air and space museum on the West Coast. Even technophobes will be engaged and delighted.**

**Flight path** The 185,075-sq ft (17,112-sq m) Museum of Flight is on the southwest corner of Boeing Field and King County International Airport, and is partly housed in the original Red Barn, where Boeing built its first planes.

**Great Gallery** The Red Barn exhibit documents early aviation up to 1938, while the airy and breathtaking Great Gallery traces the story of flight from early mythology to the latest accomplishments in space. Overhead, more than 20 full-sized airplanes hang at varying levels from a ceiling grid. All face the same direction, like a squadron frozen in flight. Another exhibit contains artifacts from the Apollo space program, including an Apollo command module, lunar rocks and the Lunar Roving Vehicle. The museum also has a full-sized air traffic control tower. Like a working tower, this simulated version overlooks airport runways and has overhead speakers that broadcast air traffic transmissions. Outside the museum building, you can tour the original Air Force One presidential jet.

**You be the pilot** In the fascinating Tower Exhibit, you can pilot an imaginary flight from Denver to Seattle to witness the behind-the-scenes work of air traffic controllers. Through visual cues on a radar screen and telephone instructions, you can perform the numerous tasks required to fly the plane, from checking weather data and filing a flight plan to landing.

### HIGHLIGHTS

- A restored 1917 Curtiss "Jenny" biplane
- A flying replica of the B&W, Boeing's first plane
- The only MD-21 Blackbird spy plane in existence
- Apollo space program artifacts
- A full-sized air traffic control tower
- Piloting an imaginary flight
- The world's first fighter, a 1914 Italian Caproni Ca 20
- Flight simulators

### INFORMATION

- 🏛 Off map M3; Locator map B4
- ✉ 9404 E Marginal Way S by Boeing Field
- ☎ 206/764–5720; www.museumofflight.or
- 🕐 Daily 10–5 (Thu till 9)
- 🍴 Wings Café
- 🚍 174
- ♿ Excellent
- 💲 Moderate. Free first Thu of month, 5–9pm
- ❓ Guided museum tours; concerts, lectures, films and special events

*A 1917 Curtiss "Jenny"*

# University of Washington

**The University campus was originally planned as a fairground for Seattle's 1909 Exposition celebrating the Alaska Gold Rush. Much of the design, including Rainier Vista—a concourse framing Mt. Rainier—has been preserved.**

**Vistas and fountains** Established in 1861 on a site in the downtown area, the university moved to its present location 30 years later. To begin your tour stop at the Visitor Information Center to pick up a free self-guided walking tour map and an events schedule. As you walk, you'll see buildings in a variety of architectural styles, from turreted Denny Hall to cathedral-like Suzzalo & Allen Library. The Suzzalo & Allen faces Red Square, a student gathering place. Only the *Broken Obelisk* sculpture and three campanile towers break the horizontal line of this plaza, which is bordered by Meany Hall, a performing arts venue.

**Elsewhere** To the west, lies the Henry Art Gallery (➤ 47). To the north, the old campus quadrangle is especially inviting in late March or early April when rows of pink Japanese cherry trees burst into bloom. Continuing toward the university's north entrance, you come to the Burke Museum (➤ 48) and UW's observatory, which is open to the public. If you head toward the Waterfront Activities building, you can rent a canoe and paddle on Lake Washington.

**The Ave** One block west of the campus lies University Avenue Northeast, known as "the Ave," the main drag through the "U district." Here, a multitude of ethnic restaurants, music and bookstores, import stores and secondhand stores share the avenue with street kids who call the neighborhood "home."

*Above: Part of the university campus. The Cascade Mountains are on the horizon*

## Henry Art Gallery

**The Henry Art Gallery expanded its gallery space in 1997 with an addition that takes advantage of the sloping site and greatly enhances the building. Today, the Henry is Seattle's leading venue for cutting-edge art.**

**The gallery** The art museum of the University of Washington has 14,000sq ft (1,302sq m) of gallery space and includes an auditorium, education studio and sculpture court that houses the elliptical Skyspace by renowned artist James Turrell.

**Skyspace** Commissioned in celebration of the Henry's 75th anniversary, the Skyspace is the first installation of its kind to combine two key aspects of Turrell's work: skyspace and exterior architectural illumination. Opened in July 2003, the artwork provides both an interior gallery experience and a public art component that can be viewed from locations outside the museum.

**The collection** Works from the permanent collection are exhibited on a rotating basis in the old building's North Gallery. A cornerstone of the collection is the Monsen Collection of Photography, prized for its scope, from vintage prints to contemporary explorations of the medium. The permanent collection also includes 19th- to 20th-century landscape painting, modern art by Stuart Davis, Robert Motherwell, Jacob Lawrence and Lionel Feininger and an extensive Native American textile collection.

**Learn as you go** In addition to films, lectures and tours, the museum presents "art dialogues"—discussions of a current exhibition—and "collection seminars" in which curators outline how an exhibition is developed and provide a behind-the-scenes look at artworks.

### DID YOU KNOW?

● Founded in 1927, the Henry was the first public art museum in the state

### HIGHLIGHTS

● The Monsen Collection of Photography
● Regular artists' lectures, symposia and film showings

### INFORMATION

✚ A5; Locator map B3
✉ UW campus at 15th Avenue, NE and NE 41st Street
☎ 206/543–2280 or 206/543–2281 (scheduled tours/events); www.henryart.org
🕐 Tue–Sun 11–5 (Thu till 8). Closed Mon and 4 July, Thanksgiving, Christmas and New Year
🍴 Gallery café
🚌 70, 71, 72, 73, 43, 25
♿ Very good
💰 Moderate; free Thu 5–8
🔗 University of Washington (➤ 46), Burke Museum (➤ 48), Arboretum (➤ 49), Museum of History and Industry (➤ 54), U District (➤ 57)
❓ Tours, lectures, discussions and special events; gallery store

47

THOMAS BURKE MEMORIAL WAS

# Burke Museum of Natural History and Culture

**The Burke's permanent collection demonstrates at once a keen artistic sense, genuine respect for the cultural traditions of featured groups and a scientist's attention to detail.**

**The Burke's beginnings** The museum's origins date back to 1879, when four enthusiastic teenagers calling themselves the Young Naturalists set about collecting Northwest plant and animal specimens, a popular hobby at the time. Their collection grew, so much that to house it a museum was built on the University of Washington campus in 1885. Over the next 20 years, the number of specimens increased, and today, they form the basis of the Burke's extensive collection, which totals more than three million objects. The museum moved into its current building in 1962.

**Treasures on display** As you walk through the entrance, a stunning glass display case demands immediate attention. It highlights selected treasures from this vast collection, and gives you an idea of what's in store. In the halls beyond, two new exhibits showcase the museum's strong suits: natural history and ethnography. The Pacific Voices exhibit conveys the variety and richness of Pacific Rim cultures, from New Zealand to the northwest coast of Canada. By framing the exhibit around the celebrations and rituals that are central to each culture, museum artifacts are placed within their appropriate context. Constructed "sets," photo murals, recorded sounds and informative text bring objects to life and communicate the importance of cultural traditions. The Life and Times of Washington State exhibit is a chronological journey through 545 million years of Washington natural history.

## DID YOU KNOW?

- The museum's anthropological division has the largest Northwest Coast collection of Indian artifacts in the western United States
- The 37,000 bird specimens in the ornithology collection account for 95 percent of North American species
- Before the Burke opened, a number of ethnic groups came to the museum for private "blessing" ceremonies to consecrate their installations

## INFORMATION

- ➕ B6; Locator map B3
- ✉ University of Washington campus at NE 45th Street and 17th Avenue NE
- ☎ 206/543–5590; www.burkemuseum.org
- 🕐 Daily 10–5 (1st Thu of month till 8)
- 🍴 Burke Café
- 🚌 70, 71, 72, 73, 43
- ♿ Very good
- 💲 Moderate. "Dollar Deal"– pay an extra dollar for same-day admission to the Henry
- ↔ University of Washington (► 46), Arboretum (► 49), Museum of History and Industry (► 54), U District (► 57)

# Washington Park Arboretum

**This large botanical collection owes its origins to Edmond S. Meany, founder of the University of Washington's School of Forestry. Today's garden combines exotics with virtually every woodland plant indigenous to the area.**

**Green oasis** Meany initiated a seed exchange with universities around the world. As a result, you can walk through a variety of ecological zones and enjoy a rich diversity of flora.

**The Japanese Garden** On the west side of Lake Washington Boulevard, tucked away behind a wooden fence, lies the restful Japanese Garden. Elements of the garden—plants, trees, water, rocks—and their placement, represent a miniature world of mountain, forest, lake, river and tableland. There's also a ceremonial teahouse.

**Waterfront trail** This 1.5-mile (2-km) trail, originating behind the Museum of History and Industry (▶ 54), winds through marshland on floating platforms and footbridges. At Foster Island, it cuts under the Evergreen Point Floating Bridge and continues through what was once a Native American burial ground to Duck Pond. To experience this convergence of man and nature from the water, rent a canoe (▶ 59) and go for a paddle through water-lilies among the mallards and their ducklings.

## DID YOU KNOW?

- Arboretum area: 200 acres (81ha)
- Botanist Edmond S. Meany test-planted imported seeds in his own garden, and later transplanted the plants on campus
- The Japanese Garden was designed in 1960 by Juki Iida, a Tokyo landscape architect, who personally supervised both its planning and construction

## INFORMATION

- ✚ B6, C6; Locator map B3
- ✉ Between E Madison Street and Hwy 520, and 26th Avenue E and Arboretum Drive E (Graham Visitor's Center at 2300 Arboretum Drive E)
- ☎ 206/543–8800; Japanese Garden 206/684–4725
- 🕐 Daily 8am to sunset; Japanese Garden daily Mar–30 Nov
- 🚌 11
- ♿ None
- 💲 Waterfront and woodland trails free; Japanese Garden free
- ↔ University of Washington (▶ 46), Museum of History and Industry (▶ 54)
- ❓ Free guided tours on weekends, year-round.

## The Boeing Tour

**Over the years, Seattle's fortunes have soared and dipped on the wings of Boeing. Touring the 747 plant and seeing workers on the job puts a human face on the region's largest employer.**

**Ceaseless activity** Thirty minutes north of Seattle, in the world's largest building measured by volume, thousands of employees go about the intricate process of assembling wide body jets. Here, 747s, 767s, and the newest, the 777, are assembled around the clock.

**The tour** The 90-minute Boeing tour begins with a short film. Afterwards, a guide takes you to the plant's third floor, where an observation deck provides a view of the final 747 assembly operation. Outside, you are shown where the painting, fueling and ground testing of the aircraft occurs.

**Company history** After flying with a barnstorming pilot at a 1915 flight show, young William Boeing was convinced of two things: He could build a better plane, and that aviation was destined for more than mere entertainment. In 1916 he and naval architect Conrad Westerveld built the B&W, the first Boeing aircraft. Following World War I, the company struggled on the verge of bankruptcy and manufactured furniture to stay afloat. Boeing's boom years commenced with the production of the B-17 bomber. Company fortunes continued to soar through the Cold War until 1969, when recession hit, but again, the company recovered. In 1996, Boeing merged with Rockwell, contractor for the US space shuttle, and in 1997, with McDonnell-Douglas, makers of the DC9. With its divisions spread further afield, Boeing announced in 2001 its plans to move corporate headquarters out of the state. Manufacturing facitilies will remain here.

### DID YOU KNOW?

- Boeing now owns Rockwell, contractor for the US space shuttle, and McDonnell Douglas, manufacturer of the DC9
- Workers use bicycles to get around the factory floor
- Boeing offers a range of customized interiors. The new 747-400s for Saudi Arabian Airlines provide curtained prayer rooms equipped with electronic devices pointing to Mecca
- The Boeing plant covers 98 acres (40ha) under one roof
- 26 overhead cranes cruise 31 miles (50km) of networked track

### INFORMATION

- Off map J3;
  Locator map C1
- ✉ Tour Center off Hwy 526 West in Everett (via I-5 northbound)
- ☎ 206/544–1264 (recording); 800/464–1746; www.boeing.com
- 🕐 Mon–Fri 8.30–4; tours at 9, 10, 11, 1, 2 and 3
- ♿ Very good
- 💲 Inexpensive
- ❓ Height restriction for children 4ft 2ins (127cms). Same-day tickets sold on-site on first-come first served basis.

# SEATTLE's
## best

51

# Parks & Beaches

## THE GREEN CITY

The city's 300 or so parks are often cited as key to Seattle's liveability. Credit goes to city officials, who feared that unchecked logging would destroy Seattle's natural beauty, and to Chicago's Olmsted Brothers Landscape Architects, who were hired to draft a comprehensive plan for the city in 1903. The system of parks and connecting boulevards they designed forms the backbone of Seattle's 5,000 acres (2,024 ha) of parkland.

*Gasworks Park*

### FREEWAY PARK

When Freeway Park opened in 1976, it won national attention for the ingenious way it created an urban oasis over ten lanes of freeway. The design called for a concrete "lid" to go over Interstate 5, pollution-resistant trees and a waterfall thundering at a rate of 27,000gal (5,940L) a minute to mask the traffic noise. Note George Tsutakawa's handsome bronze fountain.
➕ F6 ✉ 6th Avenue and Seneca Street, south of Washington State Convention Center 🚌 2

### GASWORKS PARK

This park on north Lake Union is popular for picnics, kite-flying, skateboarding and wonderful views of

downtown. Rusted, graffiti-marked towers and brightly painted machinery in the play area recall this site's origins as a gas plant. Climb the grassy mound to see the park's sundial or launch a kite.
➕ B3 ✉ N Northlake Way and Meridian Avenue N 🚌 26

### GOLDEN GARDENS BEACH PARK

This beach park is teen heaven: you'll find a half-mile strip of sandy beach and trail, views of the Olympics, a bathhouse, concessions, picnic shelters and firepits. If yachts are your thing, check out the ones next door, at Shilshole Marina. A walk along the beach at dusk is a must.
➕ Off map K2 ✉ Seaview Ave 🚌 17

### GREEN LAKE PARK

A great place to watch Seattleites doing what they like most—relax outdoors. A paved loop encircling the lake has two lanes, one for pedestrians, the other for those on wheels. Trees provide shady spots.
➕ Off map K2, L2 ✉ East Green Lake Drive (car park) 🚌 16, 26

### KERRY VIEWPOINT

This tiny park on Queen Anne Hill has a great view of downtown and features Doris Chase's steel sculpture *Changing Form*.
➕ C2 ✉ W Highland Drive and 2nd W 🚌 2 or 13

### LINCOLN PARK

In this lovely West Seattle park south of Alki, you'll find something for everyone: great views, rocky beaches with tidepools, walking and biking trails, picnic shelters, tennis courts, a horseshoe pit, a children's playground and Seattle's only outdoor saltwater pool and waterslide.
➕ Off map M2 ✉ Fauntleroy Avenue SW and SW Webster 🚌 54

### MADISON PARK

In this neighborhood beach park on the western shore of Lake Washington, you can sunbathe on a grassy slope. There's a bathhouse and a swimming dock with diving board. Lifeguards operate throughout the summer.
➕ C6 ✉ The foot of E Madison Street at 43rd Avenue E 🚌 11

### MATTHEWS BEACH

At this swimming beach on the north shore of Lake Washington, bikers on the 16.5-mile (27-km) lakeside Burke-Gilman trail stop to cool down or enjoy a picnic on the grassy meadows. There's also a playground for the children.
➕ Off map K3 ✉ NE 93rd off Sand Point Way NE 🚌 75

### SEWARD PARK

This beautiful 277-acre (112-ha) wilderness on the south shore of Lake Washington has a beach and trails along the waterfront and through old-growth cedar and fir forest (where it is sometimes possible to catch views of the two pairs of nesting eagles). It's a wonderful place for a picnic, especially if you come via bicycle on a Bicycle Saturday or Sunday, when Lake Washington is closed to traffic. Also features a fish hatchery and picnic shelters with barbecues.
➕ Off map L3 ✉ Lake Washington Boulevard S and S Juneau 🚌 39

### SEATTLE AREA BEACHES

With several freshwater lakes and miles of shoreline along Elliott Bay, Seattle boasts a number of beach parks within its city limits. However, in Seattle the term "beach" is not necessarily synonymous with "swimming." Few choose to swim in the chilly waters of Puget Sound, apart from a quick dash in and out on a hot summer's day. The freshwater of Green Lake and Lake Washington, on the other hand, are pleasant for more extended swims.

*Golden Gardens Beach Park, backed by the snow-capped Olympic Mountains*

# Greater Seattle Museums

## MUSEUM OF GLASS

Forty minutes south of Seattle lies Tacoma—home of glass artist, Dale Chihuly. In 2002 the city opened a dazzling new Museum of Glass—one of only three worldwide devoted to contemporary glass art. With 13,000sq ft (3,963m) of exhibition space, the glass-walled concrete structure incorporates in its design a 90-ft (27-m) steel cone housing the Hot Shop. There, visitors can watch workers shape enormous molten globs into art. A dramatic glass bridge with three Chihuly installations connects this museum to the Washington State History Museum across the street.

### BELLEVUE ART MUSEUM (BAM)

Across Lake Washington on Seattle's Eastside, BAM shows contemporary visual art of the Northwest. The building's sculptural qualities and architect Stephen Holl's use of natural light have created a luminous space that embodies BAM's mission of going beyond exhibition to both explore and generate art.

➕ L3 ✉ 510 Bellevue Way NE ☎ 425/519–0770; www.bellevueart.org 🕐 Tue–Sat 10–5 (Thu till 8), Sun noon–5 🚍 550 from bus tunnel 💵 Moderate

### FRYE ART MUSEUM

This beautiful, spacious gallery devoted to representational art rotates works from the permanent collection, most notably pieces by William Merritt Chase, Winslow Homer, John Singer Sargeant and Renoir.

➕ E4 ✉ 704 Terry Avenue ☎ 206/622–9250; www.fryeart.org 🕐 Tue–Sat 10–5 (Thu till 8), Sun noon–5 🍴 Café 🚍 3, 4 (on 3rd Avenue) ♿ Excellent 💵 Free ❓ Sun afternoon concerts, workshops and lectures

*An old salmon advertisement, Museum of History and Industry*

➕ N2

✉ 1801 East Dock Street, Tacoma

☎ 1–866/4–MUSEUM; www.museumofglass.org

🕐 Tue–Sat 10–5, Sun noon–5 (3rd Thu 10–8)

🍴 Prizm Café

🚂 Sounder train

🚈 Seattle express #594 Sounder train

💵 Expensive

### MUSEUM OF HISTORY AND INDUSTRY (MOHAI)

Hands-on, interactive activities, thought-provoking exhibits and an excellent collection of photographs and artifacts documenting Seattle history have made this small museum a lively learning center.

➕ B5 ✉ 2700 24th Avenue E, south of the Montlake Bridge ☎ 206/324–1126; www.seattlehistory.org 🕐 Tue–Sun 1–5; open holiday Mondays 🚍 25, 43, 48, 255 ♿ Excellent 💵 Moderate

### NORDIC HERITAGE MUSEUM

The only museum in the United States to showcase the heritage of all five Nordic nations: Denmark, Finland, Iceland, Norway and Sweden.

➕ G1 ✉ 3014 NW 67th Street ☎ 206/789–5707; www.nordicmuseum.com 🕐 Tue–Sat, 10–4, Sun noon–5 🚍 17 (on 4th Avenue) 💵 Inexpensive; free 1st Tue of month

# Public Art

### A SOUND GARDEN

One of Seattle's small treasures. Doug Hollis's ingenious work consists of 12 steel towers supporting wind activated organ pipes that create gentle sounds on windy days.

➕ C4 ✉ Behind NOAA building, 7600 Standpoint Way NE
🚌 74, 75

### DANCERS' SERIES: STEPS

At each of eight locations, Jack Mackie has fashioned cast bronze shoeprints in the pattern of a couple's feet as they dance the tango, waltz, lindy, fox trot, rhumba and mambo.

✉ Broadway on Capitol Hill 🚌 7

### FREMONT TROLL

Standing under the Aurora Avenue Bridge, this whimsical giant, who is crushing a real Volkswagen Bug with his bare hand, is both a reference to Scandinavian folklore and an expression of Fremont's collective sense of humor.

➕ A3 ✉ N 36th Street 🚌 26, 28

### OCCIDENTAL PARK TOTEMS

Duane Pasco's painted cedar logs—*Sun and Raven, Tsonqua* and *Killer Whale and Bear*—standing proud in Occidental Park, date from 1975.

➕ G6 ✉ Occidental Park, Occidental Avenue S and S Main in Pioneer Square 🚌 Buses on 1st in free zone

### RAIN FOREST GATES

Artists Jean Whitesavage and Nick Lyle creatively depict plant and animal forms of the Northwest rain forest in these forged steel gates at the corner of 2nd Avenue and South Jackson Street.

🚌 7, 14, 36

### WAITING FOR THE INTERURBAN

Richard Beyer's sculpture is a much-loved fixture of Fremont. Rarely are these gray aluminum trolley riders unadorned, either with scarves and hats in winter, or at other times through the year with balloons and banners to acknowledge someone's birthday.

➕ A3 ✉ Fremont Avenue N and N 34th Street 🚌 26, 28

## PUBLIC ART

From manhole covers and benches to bus tunnel tiles, public art is incorporated into the very fabric of Seattle's daily life. Artists worked with architects and engineers on the design for five underground stations: Convention Place, Westlake, University, Pioneer Square and the International District. The design reflects the character of each neighborhood. This art phenonemon stems from the city's May 1973 "One Percent for Art" ordinance, which specifies that 1 percent of all new municipal improvement funds must be set aside for the purchase and installation of public art. At least half of all allocations are awarded to artists residing in the Pacific Northwest. After an open call for applications selection is finalized following a review by a Seattle Arts Commission panel.

*The troll at Fremont*

# Architecture

## CHAPEL OF ST. IGNATIUS

This sublime chapel is Seattle University's architectural gift to the city. Architect Steven Holl visualized the structure as "seven bottles of light in a stone box," with light bouncing off the tinted baffles to create a halo effect on the surrounding walls.

✚ E4 ✉ 12th Avenue near Marion on Capitol Hill 🕐 Mon–Thu 7am–10pm, Fri 7–7, Sat 9–5, Sun 9–11. Regular liturgies ☎ 206/296–5587 🚌 2, 12

*The ornate interior of the 5th Avenue Theater*

## FIFTH AVENUE THEATER

Built in 1926, this ornately carved theater is patterned after the imperial throne room in Beijing's Forbidden City.

✚ F6 ✉ 1308 5th Avenue ☎ 206/625–1418 🚌 Downtown free zone buses along 1st to 4th Avenue

## HARBOR STEPS

In creating a pedestrian link between the Waterfront and 1st Avenue Vancouver architect Arthur Anderson crafted an inviting urban plaza with waterfalls, seating and plantings.

✚ F6 ✉ University Avenue 🚌 Downtown free zone buses along 1st to 4th Avenue

## SMITH TOWER

When it opened in 1914, Smith Tower was Seattle's first steel-framed skyscraper and the tallest building outside of New York City. At 42 stories, it remained the tallest building west of the Mississippi until 1969. For a modest fee, you can ride to the 35th floor in the company of the last of Seattle's elevator attendants to get a sweeping view of downtown.

✉ 506 2nd Avenue and Yesler Way

## SECURITY PACIFIC BANK TOWER

Architect Minoru Yamasaki once said that he tried to create "delight, serenity and surprise" in his buildings. This inverted white pencil, balanced on a 12-story base, clearly succeeds at the very least on the last count.

✚ F6 ✉ 1200 4th Avenue between Union and University 🚌 Downtown free zone buses along 1st to 4th Avenue

## WASHINGTON MUTUAL BUILDING

As critics lambasted this late 1980s Kohn Pederson Fox building as an Empire State clone, the public applauded the postmodern style as relief from the cold glass boxes that dominate downtown.

✚ F6 ✉ 1201 3rd Avenue 🚌 Downtown free zone buses along 1st to 4th Avenue

# Neighborhoods

## BELLTOWN

This unconventional neighborhood north of the Market is an odd mix of seediness and gentrification. The area's working-class roots are still evident even as upscale restaurants and condos, cyber-cafés and taverns with art on the walls have transformed and energized the neighborhood.
🚌 Buses on 1st and 3rd

## CAPITOL HILL

Diverse and progressive, two miles (3km) east of downtown, Capitol Hill is the focal point of the Seattle gay community, and home to a smattering of Seattle's monied elite as well as young professionals and seniors on fixed incomes. The action is concentrated along Broadway in cafés, restaurants, retro stores and clubs.
🚌 7 to Broadway E, or 10 to 15th Avenue E

## FREMONT

This offbeat neighborhood, which proclaims itself a republic and "the Center of the Universe," is known for its tolerance and quirky humor. Check out the public art, from the monumental statue of Lenin to the Volkswagen-crushing *Fremont Troll* under Aurora Bridge.
🚌 26, 28

## MADISON PARK

This older residential neighborhood bordering Lake Washington at the foot of Madison boasts lovely homes, a popular beach (► 53) and a cluster of interesting specialty stores and cafés.
🚌 11 to the foot of Madison

## UNIVERSITY DISTRICT

This area includes the University of Washington (► 46), "the Ave," and University Village, a complex of tasteful specialty stores, markets and cafés. "The Ave" is full of student haunts, ethnic restaurants and interesting shops—including the awesome and justifiably renowned University Bookstore (► 76).
🚌 Many including 7, 43, 70, 71,72, 73, 85

**FREMONT FOLLIES**

Seattle has earned its "most liveable city" moniker through the strength and character of its neighborhoods, of which Fremont, where tongue-in-cheek irreverence runs high, ranks as the quirkiest. In Fremont, bumper-stickers that elsewhere in the United States read: "HONK IF YOU LOVE JESUS;" instead ask you to: "HONK IF YOU *ARE* JESUS."

*Artistic graffiti in Fremont*

# Active Pursuits

## SEATTLE BY BIKE

Despite the omnipresent threat of drizzle and the challenge of hilly terrain, growing numbers of Seattleites are taking to two wheels for commuting and recreation. The city is laced with bike trails, including a number of flat, scenic routes that reward bikers and in-line skaters with spectacular views.

*Exploring Seattle by bike*

## DID YOU SAY "BIKE?"

For those who associate "bike" with Harley, Seattle's downtown Harley-Davidson store provides daily and weekend rentals from late spring into the fall for those 25 and older with a motorcycle credential.
✉ 206/243–5000;
www.downtownharley.com

### BIKE TRAILS

• Alki Beach to Lincoln Park: This flat bikeway is marked only part of the way; continue along the shoreline to Lincoln Park for a 12-mile (19-km) round trip.
🚌 37 (daytime only), 56

• Burke-Gilman Trail: This flat 16.5-mile (27-km), paved, lakeside trail follows an old railroad right-of-way, skirting Fremont, Wallingford and the University of Washington campus. From Fremont/Ballard, the trail runs east along the ship canal, Lake Union and Portage Bay. At the University of Washington's Husky Stadium, the trail swings north along Lake Washington and continues for 12 miles (19km) to the northern tip of the lake at Kenmore. If you want to go to the Woodinville Wineries and Brewpub, pick up the Sammamish River Trail.

• Lake Washington Boulevard. In summer on Bicycle Saturdays and Sundays, traffic is barred from a 6-mile (10-km) stretch of Lake Washington Boulevard, between the arboretum and Lake Washington and south along the lake to Seward Park. (Mostly flat with one hill.) This part joins Seward Park's 2.5 mile (4km) loop. (▶ 53)
☎ Bicycle Sat/Sun Schedule: 206/684–4075

• Magnolia Bluff Bike Trail: 3 miles (5km) from Discovery Park to Magnolia Park with views of Elliott Bay, Mt. Rainier and downtown. Moderate with one steep hill.
🚌 24, 33

### BIKE & IN-LINE SKATE RENTALS

• Gregg's Green Lake Cycle: rents in-line skates, skateboards and snowboards.
➕ A6 ✉ 7007 Woodlawn Avenue NE ☎ 206/523–1822; www.greggscycles.com 🕐 Mon–Fri 10–9, Sat–Sun 10–6

• Montlake Bicycle Shop: rents bikes and bike trailers.
➕ C5 ✉ 2223 24th Avenue E (near the Arboretum)
☎ 206/329–7333; www.montlakebike.com 🕐 Mon–Fri 10–7, Sat 9–5, Sun 10–4 🚌 43

• Urban Surf In-line Skate Rental: Opposite Gasworks Park on the Burke-Gilman trail, this shop rents in-line skates, helmets, knee, wrist and elbow pads.
➕ B3 ✉ 210 N Northlake Way ☎ 206/545–9463; www.urbansurf.com 🕓 Mon–Fri 10–7, Sat 10–5, Sun 11–5

**BOAT RENTALS**
• Agua Verde Paddle Club: hourly kayak rentals from its boathouse and tasty, economical Mexican eats and drinks up above.
➕ A4 ✉ 1303 NE Boat Street (on Portage Bay)
☎ 206/545–8570 🕓 Mon–Sat 10–dusk, Sun 10–6
• Green Lake Boat Rentals: paddleboats and rowboats.
➕ A6 ✉ 7351 E Green Lake Drive N
☎ 206/527–0171 🕓 Mon–Fri 11–6, Sat–Sun 10–6 (weather permitting) 🚌 26
• On Lake Washington/Portage Bay: try UW Waterfront Activities Center for canoes and rowboats.
✉ Waterfront Activities Building ☎ 206/543–9433
🕓 Mon–Fri 10 till one hour before dusk 🚌 25, 43
• On Lake Union: Center for Wooden Boats for sailboats and rowboats; also a classic wooden boat museum.
➕ B3 ✉ 1010 Valley Street ☎ 206/382–2628; www.cwb.org 🕓 Daily 11–7, May–Oct; 11–5, rest of year 🚌 17
• Moss Bay Rowing and Kayak Center: kayaks and shells—lessons, tours, rentals.
➕ C4 ✉ 1001 Fairview Avenue N #1900 🕓 Daily 8am–8pm; shorter hours in winter ☎ 206/682–2031; www.mossbay.net 🚌 70, 71, 72, 73
• Northwest Marine Charters: bare boat rental and skippered outings.
➕ B3 ✉ 2520 Westlake N ☎ 206/283–3040 🕓 Call for appointment 🚌 17
• NW Outdoor Center: kayaks, also classes, day trips.
➕ B3 ✉ 2100 Westlake Avenue N ☎ 206/281–9694; www.nwoc.com 🚌 17
• Wind Works Sailing Center: bare boat or skippered charters.
➕ G1 ✉ 7001 Seaview NW, Suite 133 ☎ 206/784–9386; www.sail1.com 🕓 Thu–Tue 9–5, Oct to mid-Apr

**FISHING**
• A Spot Tail Salmon Guide: Salmon fishing in Puget Sound with guide tackle and fishing license provided.
➕ Off map ✉ Shilshole Marina, Ballard ☎ 206/283–6680; www.salmonguide.com 🕓 Call for appointment 🚌 #18

**GOLF COURSES**
• Jackson Park
➕ Off map ✉ NE 135th and 10th Avenue NE, off I-5
☎ 206/363–4747 🚌 73
• Jefferson Park
➕ G4 ✉ 4101 Beacon Avenue S ☎ 206/762–9949 🚌 36
• West Seattle Golf Course
➕ Off map ✉ 4470 35th SW ☎ 206/935–5187 🚌 21, 22, 54, 55

*Canoeing on Lake Union*

**THE BURKE-GILMAN TRAIL: HIGHLIGHTS**

● Fremont neighborhood
● Gasworks Park
● University of Washington campus
● University Village
● Sound Garden public art (nearby)
● Matthews Beach (extension to Sammamish River Trail)
● Woodinville Wineries
● Redhook Brewery, Woodinville

59

# What's Free & Nearly Free

## MICROSOFT MUSEUM

Those fascinated with Microsoft's meteoric rise can visit the free Microsoft Museum across Lake Washington on Seattle's Eastside. Located in Redmond, adjacent to the main campus and corporate headquarters, the museum recounts 28 years of software history and features artifacts like the world's first personal computer. In addition, interactive exhibits allow visitors to try out Microsoft's latest products, including new Xbox titles and pc games.
✉ 4420 148th Avenue NE, Building 1217, Redmond
☎ 425/703–6214
🕙 Mon–Fri 9–7, closed for occasional private events
🎫 Free

*Seattle Asian Art Museum*

### In the Top 25

1 **DISCOVERY PARK & DAYBREAK STAR ART CENTER (► 26)**
11 **FERRY TO BAINBRIDGE ISLAND (► 36)**
4 **FISHERMEN'S TERMINAL (► 29)**
16 **KLONDIKE GOLD RUSH NATIONAL HISTORIC PARK(► 41)**
3 **THE HIRAM M. CHITTENDEN LOCKS (► 28)**
10 **PIKE PLACE MARKET (► 35)**
17 **REI (► 42)**
13 **VOLUNTEER PARK (► 44)**

## COAST GUARD MUSEUM

On pier 36, the museum features a collection of navigational aids, ships models and various maritime artifacts explaining the history and of the Coast Guard.
✚ F3 ✉ Pier 36 on waterfront ☎ 206/217–6993 🕙 Mon, Wed, Fri, 9–3, Sat–Sun 1–5

## CONVENTION CENTER GALLERIES

The North Galleria has an outstanding permanent collection and rotating displays on loan featuring Northwest painting, sculpture, ceramic and glass art.
✚ E6 ✉ 800 Convention Place ☎ 206/693–5000 🕙 Daily 7am–10pm

## GLASSHOUSE STUDIO LTD

Watch glass-blowers at work in this Pioneer Square studio adjacent to the large gallery.
✚ G6 ✉ 311 Occidental Avenue S ☎ 206/682–9939
🕙 Mon–Sat 10–5, Sun 11–4 🚌 Any buses on 1st (free zone)

## HISTORY HOUSE

Depicts the history of Seattle neighborhoods with photo displays, interactive kiosks and animated slide shows. Also features a small sculpture garden.
✚ A2 ✉ 790 N 34th Street, Fremont ☎ 206/675–8875;
www.historyhouse.org 🕙 Wed–Sun noon–5

## LAKE VIEW CEMETERY

Seattle's pioneers are buried here, but it's the graves of martial arts cult star Bruce Lee (near the top of the hill) and his son, Brandon, that draw visitors.
✚ C4, C5 ✉ 1554 15th Avenue East at E Garfield, Capitol Hill 🚌 10

## VOLUNTEER PARK WATER TOWER

Best free view of the city.
✚ C4, C5 ✉ West of 15th Avenue E between E Prospect and E Galer
🚌 10

## WOODLAND PARK ROSE GARDEN

Over 5,000 roses here normally peak in early July.
✚ Off map ✉ 5500 Phinney Avenue N 🚌 5 (from 3rd and Pine)

# Free Events

### ART WALKS
• On the first Thursday of the month, Pioneer Square art galleries stay open from 5–8pm for the monthly gallery stroll. The event attracts both collectors and those who come for the scene.
• Across Lake Washington, Kirkland's downtown area has its own gallery walk on the second Thursday of the month.

### BREWERY TOURS
• Pyramid Breweries: Daily tours, with samples of Pyramid Ales and Thomas Kemper lagers and sodas.
➕ A5 ✉ 1201 1st Avenue S ☎ 206/682–3377 🖥 Downtown free zone
• Redhook Ale Brewery: The first in Seattle with craft brews. Daily tours at Woodinville facility, 25 minutes northeast of Seattle.
➕ Off map ✉ Woodinville ☎ 425/483-3232

### CULTURAL FESTIVALS
Seattle Center hosts a year-long series of weekend festivals celebrating the cultural heritages of Seattle's major ethnic communities. Often coordinated with special holidays like Vietnamese New Year.
☎ 206/684–7200 or 206/684–8582 (recorded message)

### ELLIOTT BAY BOOK COMPANY READINGS
This first-rate bookstore has a program of readings by noted authors six days a week, usually free. Café.
➕ G6 ✉ 101 S Main Street ☎ 206/624–6600 (ticket information) 🖥 Downtown free zone

### FREMONT SUNDAY MARKETS
Fresh produce, flowers, crafts, collectibles, antiques and plain old junk.
➕ A2 ✉ Fremont neighborhood on N 34th between Stone Way and Fremont Avenue N 🕒 Sun 10–4, May–Oct

### FRYE MUSEUM EVENTS
Lectures, workshops and classical music concerts on Sunday afternoons.
➕ E4 ✉ 704 Terry Avenue ☎ 206/622–9250 🚌 3, 4, 12

### UNIVERSITY DISTRICT FARMERS' MARKET
Flowers and farm fresh produce, summer Saturdays.
➕ A6 ✉ University Way NE and NE 50th 🚌 70, 71, 72, 73, 43

### CHATEAU STE. MICHELLE
Daily tours and wine tastings 10–4.30. Picnic area. Reservations and small fee required for special vintage-reserve room tastings.
➕ Off map ✉ 14111 NE 145th Street in Woodinville, NE of Seattle
☎ 425/415–3300 🚌 255 to Kingsgate then short walk

### SEAFAIR

Each summer, a series of over 50 community events take place between mid-July and early August. Known as "Seafair," the festivities range from children's parades and Native American pow-wows to the legendary Torchlight Parade and hydroplane races. A number of Seafair's public events are free.
☎ 206/728–0123; www.seafair.org

### HANDMADE BREWS

Seattles brewers have pioneered the US's move away from mass-produced beers to more subtly flavored "craft brews." With at least eight brewpubs in the area, some call Seattle "the microbrew capital of the world."

# For Kids

*Cooling off Seattle-style*

### In the Top 25

- **23 BURKE MUSEUM (► 48)**
- **11 FERRY TO BAINBRIDGE ISLAND (► 36)**
- **16 LAKE UNION (► 39)**
- **20 MUSEUM OF FLIGHT (► 45)**
- **6 PACIFIC SCIENCE CENTER (► 31)**
- **17 REI (► 42)**
- **9 THE WATERFRONT & AQUARIUM (► 34)**
- **5 WOODLAND PARK ZOO (► 30)**

### CHILDREN'S MUSEUM

A magical world where toddlers and young children can shop for groceries in a child-sized market, visit an African village or create enormous soap bubbles.
➕ D2 ✉ The Center House, first level, Seattle Center ☎ 206/441–1768; www.thechildrensmuseum.org ⏰ Mon–Fri 10–5, Sat–Sun 10–6 🚌 3, 4, 16, 24, 33 to Seattle Center; monorail from downtown

### FUN FOREST AMUSEMENT PARK

Rides, carnival games and cotton candy.
➕ D3 ✉ Seattle Center ☎ 206/728–1585 ⏰ Daily noon–11, Jun–Aug; off season hours vary 🚌 3, 4, 16 to Seattle Center

### GAMEWORKS

Video arcade for the 21st century.
➕ F6 ✉ 1511 7th Avenue ☎ 206/521–0952; www.gameworks.com

### NW PUPPET CENTER

Multicultural stories from around the world. Productions by the award-winning Carter Family Marionettes, the resident company and by guest companies from all over the globe. Theater includes small exhibit area. Seven different productions, Oct–May and summer tours.
➕ A5 ✉ 9123 15th Avenue NE ☎ 206/523–2579; www.nwpuppet.org 🚌 73, 77, 78

### ODYSSEY MARITIME DISCOVERY CENTER

Three state-of-the-art exhibits highlight the working waterfront: You can board a "virtual kayak" and negotiate the Puget Sound inlets, while Harvesting the Sea gives you the opportunity to skipper a commercial fishing boat, and the Ocean Trade gallery allows you to load a container vessel and measure yourself against the pros.
➕ D3 ✉ Bell Harbor's Pier 66 ☎ 206/374–4000; www.ody.org 🚋 Waterfront streetcar

### SEATTLE CHILDREN'S THEATER

Recognized worldwide for its innovative programing, SCT is a prized cultural resource for families.
➕ D2 ✉ Seattle Center ☎ 206/441–3322; www.sct.org ⏰ Performances Fri–Sun, Sep–Jun 🚌 1, 2, 3, 4, 16, 24, 33 to Seattle Center

## A GREAT PLACE FOR KIDS

In the 1980's, Seattle launched a major effort to create a more "child-friendly" urban environment that would discourage the exodus of middle class families to the suburbs. The city joined forces with civic groups to create an abundance of outdoor recreation and entertainment venues.

# SEATTLE
## where to...

# Northwest Classics & American Cuisine

## PRICES

Expect to pay per person for a meal, excluding drinks:

$ = Under $15
$$ = $15 to $30
$$$ = over $30

## NORTHWEST CLASSICS

### CAMPAGNE ($$$)

Award-winning country-French fare in the heart of the Pike Place Market featuring one of the city's best wine lists.
✚ F5 ✉ 86 Pine Street
☎ 206/728–2800
🕐 Dinner nightly

### CANLIS ($$$)

Excellent Northwest fare with Asian accents. A special occasion eatery.
✚ A3 ✉ 2576 Aurora Avenue N ☎ 206/283–3313
🕐 Dinner Mon–Sat

### CASCADIA ($$$)

Chef and owner, Kerry Sear, has won raves for the Northwest cuisine at his Belltown restaurant. Sear puts a fresh twist on local ingredients, creating utterly original fare like Douglas fir sorbet.
✚ D3 ✉ 2328 1st Avenue
☎ 206/448–8884 🕐 Dinner Mon–Sat

### DAHLIA LOUNGE ($$)

Innovative Northwest cuisine in lively, colorful surroundings.
✚ E6 ✉ 2001 4th Avenue
☎ 206/682–4142 🕐 Lunch Mon–Fri, dinner nightly

### LE GOURMAND ($$$)

For more than two decades this hard-to-find French-Northwest spot has been making locals swoon.
✚ G1 ✉ 425 NW Market Street ☎ 206/784–3463
🕐 Dinner Wed–Sat

### THE HERBFARM ($$$)

Reservations are essential if you want to eat at this legendary, award-winning restaurant serving seasonal Northwest cuisine.
✚ Off map ✉ 14580 NE 145th Street (at Willows Lodge)
☎ 206/784–2222

### THE METROPOLITAN GRILL ($$$)

Stellar steaks and legendary martinis draw crowds nightly. Happy hour features inexpensive food specials in the bar, where stogies are encouraged.
✚ F6 ✉ 820 2nd Avenue
☎ 206/624–3287 🕐 Lunch Mon–Fri, dinner nightly

### PALISADE ($$$)

Polynesian cocktails, an indoor fish pond and a view of moored sailboats on Puget Sound outside make this a popular place for a special occasion.
✚ D2 ✉ 2601 W Marina Place ☎ 206/285–1000
🕐 Lunch Mon–Fri, dinner nightly, brunch on weekends

### ROVER'S ($$$)

Often credited with serving the first haute cuisine in Seattle, the menu is full of truffles and *fois gras*.
✚ C6 ✉ 2808 E Madison Street ☎ 206/325–7442
🕐 Dinner Tue–Sat

### SALISH LODGE RESTAURANT ($$$)

Perched above Snoqualmie Falls, the cozy interiors of the restaurant offer stunning views and the menu features artful Northwest fare.
✚ Off map ✉ 6501 Railroad Avenue SE, Snoqualmie
☎ 800/826–6124
🕐 Breakfast, lunch and dinner daily, brunch on weekends

### SKYCITY AT THE NEEDLE ($$$)

At 500ft (152m) above Seattle, the pricey dinners are only average, but the view is priceless.

🕂 D3 ✉ 219 4th Avenue N (in the Space Needle) ☎ 206/905–2173 ⏱ Lunch and dinner daily, brunch on weekends

### SZMANIA'S ($$)

This once ground-breaking restaurant is now a neighborhood spot filled with loyal regulars.

🕂 E6 ✉ 3321 W McGraw Street ☎ 206/284–7305 ⏱ Dinner Tue–Sat

## AMERICAN CUISINE

### 5 SPOT ($)

An ever-changing menu that concentrates on different regions every few months: You never know if you'll get Creole catfish or New England clam chowder.

🕂 B2 ✉ 1502 Queen Anne Avenue N ☎ 206/285–7768 ⏱ Breakfast, lunch and dinner daily

### HATTIE'S HAT ($)

One of Seattle's oldest and proudest diners pours a stiff drink and cooks up some mean comfort food.

🕂 Off map ✉ 5231 Ballard Avenue NW ☎ 206/784–0175 ⏱ Dinner nightly, brunch on weekends

### HILLTOP ALE HOUSE ($)

This neighborhood eatery is great for catching a game and does better-than-pub grub with a variety of microbrews on tap.

🕂 C2 ✉ 2129 Queen Anne Avenue N ☎ 206/285–3877 ⏱ Lunch and dinner daily

### PALACE KITCHEN ($$$)

Urban American dining at its best. High-ceilings and dim lighting make the gas station, uniform-clad cooks in the open kitchen even more fun to watch.

🕂 E5 ✉ 2030 5th Avenue ☎ 206/448–2001 ⏱ Lunch Mon–Fri, dinner nightly

### RED MILL BURGERS ($)

Truly great burgers, shakes and onion rings. Kid-friendly, but it's such a great place to eat that it's usually packed with adults. Two locations.

🕂 G2; A1 ✉ 312 N 67th Street; 1613 W Dravus Street ☎ 206/783–6262; 206/284–6363 ⏱ Lunch and dinner Tue–Sun

### SHULTZY'S SAUSAGE ($)

This modest, University district eatery features their signature sausages, made from high-quality ingredients, plus a rotating menu of beers. Other menu items include veggie burgers and a chicken sandwich. Shultzy's has a loyal following whose photos decorate the walls.

🕂 A5 ✉ 4114 University Way NE ☎ 206/548–9461 ⏱ Lunch and dinner daily

### SIX ARMS ($)

Microbrews on tap and tasty burgers and fries in a laid-back, comfortable, neighborhood pub that also has spacious wooden booths.

🕂 E6 ✉ 300 E Pike Street ☎ 206/223–1698 ⏱ Lunch and dinner daily

### FARESTART ($–$$)

This non-profit restaurant serves delicious, hearty meals at budget prices while training homeless men and women for jobs in the food service industry. The weekday lunch buffet, which includes a range of remarkably ambitious preparations, is popular and on Thursday nights, when top chefs from local restaurants prepare outstanding dinners. There's a fixed price for full-course meals and all proceeds are plowed back into the program.

🕂 E5 ✉ 1902 2nd Avenue ⏱ Lunch Mon–Fri, dinner Thu only ☎ 206/443–1233

# Seafood & Vegetarian

## SEAFOOD

### BROOKLYN SEAFOOD, STEAK & OYSTER BAR ($$)

The perfect place for slurping cool oysters and sipping ice-cool Martinis.

✚ F5 ✉ 1212 2nd Avenue ☎ 206/224–7000 🕐 Lunch Mon–Sat, dinner nightly

### THE CRAB POT ($$)

The waterfront location and come-as-you-are appeal is perfect for families. Don a bib and crack your crab right on the paper-lined tables.

✚ D3 ✉ 1301 Alaskan Way (Pier 57) ☎ 206/624–1890 🕐 Lunch and dinner daily

### CUTTERS ($$$)

Family-friendly seafood dining at the north end of Pike Place Market.

✚ D3 ✉ 2001 Western Avenue ☎ 206/448–4884 🕐 Lunch and dinner daily, brunch Sun

### ETTA'S SEAFOOD ($$)

Located just outside of Pike Place Market, Seattle restaurateur Tom Douglas' ode to seafood with an Asian, innovative bent is a favorite with the crowds.

✚ E5 ✉ 2020 Western Avenue ☎ 206/443–6000 🕐 Lunch and dinner daily, brunch on weekends

### FLYING FISH ($$)

Hip, stylish, approachable and always packed. Expect unusual fish and fun preparation: Don't miss the family-style fish tacos.

✚ E5 ✉ 2234 1st Avenue ☎ 206/728–8595 🕐 Dinner daily

### ANTHONY'S HOMEPORT RESTAURANTS ($$)

Airy and attractive restaurants each afford fine waterfront views and fresh seafood, salads and desserts. Full bar.

✚ D3 ✉ 2201 Alaskan Way (Pier 66) ☎ 206/448–6688 ✚ G1 ✉ At Shilshole in Ballard, 6135 Seaview NW ☎ 206/783–0780

### STEAMERS SEAFOOD CAFÉ ($)

This informal waterfront café boasts great fish 'n chips, steamer clams and other Northwest specialties. Beer and wine. Outside seating during summer months.

✚ D3 ✉ 1200 Alaskan Way (Pier 56) ☎ 206/623–2066

### IVAR'S ($)

Ask anyone for fish 'n' chips in Seattle and they'll send you to Ivar's. The casual fish bars are ideal for an easy lunch.

✚ D3 ✉ 1001 Alaskan Way (Pier 54) ☎ 206/624–6852 🕐 Lunch and dinner daily

### JACK'S FISH SPOT ($)

Locals know this is the place to go for great cioppino and fresh fish 'n' chips.

✚ E3 ✉ 1514 Pike Place ☎ 206/467–0514 🕐 Lunch daily

### PALISADE ($$$)

Seafood with Polynesian flare and a stunning waterfront location make this place a special occasion must.

✚ Off map ✉ 2601 W Marine Place ☎ 206/285–1000 🕐 Lunch and dinner daily, brunch on weekends

### RAY'S BOATHOUSE ($$$)

A to-die-for view and dependably good seafood are the draws at this lively fish house. The upstairs café offers a waterside outdoor deck and plenty of people-watching.

✚ G1 ✉ 6049 Seaview Avenue NW ☎ 206/789–3770 🕐 Lunch and dinner daily

### RESTAURANT ZOE ($$)

Set in the heart of Seattle's hip Belltown neighborhood, young, beautiful and discerning diners pack the room for expertly prepared fish and seafood, and fun cocktails.

✚ E5 ✉ 2137 2nd Avenue ☎ 206/256–2060 🕐 Dinner Mon–Sat

### SALTY'S ON ALKI ($$-$$$)

There's simply no better view of the stunning Seattle skyline. Features approachable seafood preparations and a famous Sunday brunch.

➕ Off map ✉ 1936 Harbor Avenue SW ☎ 206/937–1600 🕐 Lunch, dinner and brunch daily

### THIRD FLOOR FISH CAFÉ ($$)

Set three floors above the shores of Lake Washington in Kirkland, this smart fish house offers some of the best seafood around.

➕ Off map ✉ 205 Lake Street, Kirkland ☎ 425/822–3553 🕐 Dinner nightly

### WATERFRONT ($$$)

Asian-accented fine dining worthy of locals and tourists alike on the breathtaking shores of Lake Union. The outdoor, waterside seating is the best place in town for sunset gazing.

➕ D2 ✉ 2801 Alaskan Way (Pier 70) ☎ 206/956–9171 🕐 Dinner nightly

## VEGETARIAN

### CAFÉ AMBROSIA ($$$)

Chic, all-organic vegan cuisine on the shores of Lake Union.

➕ B4 ✉ 2501 Fairview Avenue E ☎ 206/325–7111 🕐 Dinner Tue–Sun, brunch Sun

### CAFÉ FLORA ($$)

A glass-lined atrium dining room sets the stage for harmonious meat-free fare. Sunday brunches are very popular here so call and make a reservation.

➕ F6 ✉ 2901 Madison Street ☎ 206/325–9100 🕐 Lunch Tue–Fri, dinner Tue–Sun, brunch on weekends

### CARMELITA ($$)

Creative and innovative dining set in the charming Phinney Ridge neighborhood. Outdoor seating is available.

➕ A2 ✉ 7314 Greenwood Avenue N ☎ 206/706–7703 🕐 Dinner Tue–Sun

### FLOWERS ($)

Funky, laid-back college bar with a terrific vegetarian lunch buffet.

➕ A6 ✉ 4247 University Way NE ☎ 206/633–1903 🕐 Lunch and dinner daily

### GRAVITY BAR ($)

Menu consists of mostly vegan dishes and the friendly staff will amend non-vegan dishes to suit.

➕ D4 ✉ 415 Broadway E ☎ 206/325–7186 🕐 Lunch and dinner daily

### GREEN CAT CAFÉ ($)

Urban vegetarian coffee shop with terrific daily specials and tasty morning fare.

➕ D4 ✉ 1514 E Olive Way ☎ 206/726–8756 🕐 Breakfast and lunch daily

### STILL LIFE ($)

A living room of artsy folks sipping coffee and noshing on veg-friendly vittles.

➕ A2 ✉ 705 N 35th Street ☎ 206/547–9850 🕐 Breakfast, lunch and dinner daily

67

# Asian/Sushi

## SUPER SUSHI

### I LOVE SUSHI ($$)
Popular, crowded sushi bar on the shores of Lake Union.
🔂 B4 ✉ 1001 Fairview Avenue ☎ 206/625–9604 ⏰ Lunch Mon–Fri, dinner nightly

### SANMI SUSHI ($$)
This tiny, unassuming eatery next to Palisades on Magnolia's Smith Cove has, some say, the best sushi in town. Beer, wine and sake.
🔂 D2 ✉ 2601 Marina Place ☎ 206/283–9978 ⏰ Lunch Mon–Fri, dinner nightly
🚌 19, 24

### SHIRO'S SUSHI ($$)
Immaculate sushi served in a crisp setting. Sit at the bar for the ultimate experience.
🔂 D3 ✉ 2401 2nd Avenue ☎ 206/443–9844 ⏰ Dinner nightly

### CHINA GATE ($$)
International District restaurant decorated with golden dragons, reputed to have some of the best dim sum. Extensive menu including a variety of seafood.
🔂 E4 ✉ 516 7th Avenue S ☎ 206/624–1730 ⏰ Lunch and dinner daily

### DRAGONFISH ASIAN CAFÉ ($$)
A fun eatery with lively appetizers and specialty martinis in the heart of the hotel district.
🔂 E6 ✉ 722 Pine Street ☎ 206/467–7777 ⏰ Lunch and dinner daily

### KAU KAU BARBECUE ($)
Addictive roast duck and barbecued pork. Take it to go as ambience is lacking.
🔂 E4 ✉ 656 S King Street ☎ 206/682–4006 ⏰ Lunch and dinner daily

### KRITTIKA NOODLES AND THAI ($)
Crowds line up for the terrific Thai at this spot in the heart of the Green Lake neighborhood.
🔂 Off map ✉ 6411 Latona Avenue NE ☎ 206/985–1182 ⏰ Lunch Mon–Fri, dinner nightly

### MALAY SATAY HUT ($)
Authentic Malaysian food that has locals lining up nightly for a daring taste of something different.
🔂 F4 ✉ 212 12th Avenue S ☎ 206/324–4091 ⏰ Lunch Mon–Fri, dinner nightly

### NOODLE RANCH ($)
Tasty pan-Asian fare with the emphasis on noodles, at affordable prices.
🔂 E5 ✉ 2228 2nd Avenue ☎ 206/728–0463 ⏰ Lunch and dinner Mon–Sat

### NISHINO ($$)
Impeccable sushi and terrific *omakase* (chef-designed prix-fixe dinners) in elegant, soothing surroundings.
🔂 F6 ✉ 3130 Madison Street ☎ 206/322–5800 ⏰ Dinner nightly

### OHANA ($–$$)
This Belltown eatery offers delicious Asian food with a Hawaiian twist served in a funky, faux tropical setting. Cocktails; sushi bar.
🔂 E5 ✉ 2207 1st Avenue ☎ 206/956–9329 ⏰ Lunch Tue–Fri, dinner nightly

### SHANGHAI GARDEN CHINESE RESTAURANT ($$)
In the heart of the International District. An endless menu features fresh seafood and exotic ingredients.
🔂 E4 ✉ 524 6th Avenue S ☎ 206/625–1689 ⏰ Lunch and dinner daily

### TYPHOON ($$)
Intriguing menu choice and delicious Thai cuisine in a setting of old photographs and Thai antiques.
🔂 F5 ✉ 1400 Western Avenue ☎ 206/262–9797 ⏰ Lunch Mon–Sat, dinner nightly

### WILD GINGER ($$)
The most popular and perhaps most lauded restaurant in Seattle serving legendary Fragrant Duck, with a bar that's bulging with beautiful people.
🔂 F6 ✉ 1401 3rd Avenue ☎ 206/623–4450 ⏰ Dinner nightly

# Mexican/Nuevo-Latino

### EL CAMINO ($$)
Lively crowds pack this Fremont neighborhood spot for Mexican fare and tasty margaritas.

🔲 A3 ✉ 607 N 35th Street
☎ 206/632–7303 🕐 Dinner nightly; closed Labor Day

### FANDANGO ($$)
Excellent Mexican with polish. The bar attracts well-dressed 30-somethings for *tapas* and cocktails.

🔲 G3 ✉ 2313 1st Avenue
☎ 206/441–1188
🕐 Dinner nightly

### HARVEST VINE ($$)
A tiny neighborhood best-kept-secret with some of the best *tapas* in the city and a line every night.

🔲 F6 ✉ 2701 Madison Street
☎ 206/320–9771 🕐 Dinner Tue–Sat

### MAMA'S MEXICAN KITCHEN ($)
The funky crowds of Belltown head here for inexpensive Mexican fare and sip cocktails amid the kitschy decor.

🔲 D3 ✉ 2234 2nd Avenue
☎ 206/728–6262 🕐 Lunch and dinner daily

### TANGO TAPAS RESTAURANT & LOUNGE ($$)
Stylish dining on the edge of Seattle's Capitol Hill neighborhood.

🔲 E6 ✉ 1100 Pike Street
☎ 206/583–0382
🕐 Dinner nightly

### TAQUERIA GUAYMAS ($)
Authentic and delicious Mexican food on Capitol Hill at bargain prices.

🔲 D4 ✉ 213 Broadway E
☎ 206/860–7345 🕐 Lunch and dinner daily

## ITALIAN/ MEDITERRANEAN

### ASSAGGIO ($$)
Lively, spirited and always packed. Pastas are terrific, but can be bested by daily specials.

🔲 E5 ✉ 2010 4th Avenue
☎ 206/441–1399 🕐 Lunch Mon–Fri, dinner Mon–Sat

### BRASA ($$–$$$)
Award-winning chef specialties include grilled and wood-fired selections infused with the flavors of the Mediterranean.

🔲 D4 ✉ 2107 3rd Avenue
☎ 206/728–4220
🕐 Dinner nightly

### CAFÉ JUANITA ($$$)
A perennial favorite that just keeps getting better, this quiet Kirkland spot is worth the drive from Seattle.

🔲 Off map ✉ 9702 NE 120th Place, Kirkland ☎ 425/823–1505 🕐 Dinner Tue–Sun

### IL TERRAZZO CARMINE ($$$)
A Seattle institution worthy of its reputation. Some of the best Italian food in the city awaits.

🔲 F3 ✉ 411 1st Avenue S
☎ 206/467–7797 🕐 Lunch Mon–Fri, dinner Mon–Sat

### MACHIAVELLI ($$)
Casual and inexpensive; tasty pastas served on tables laid with checkered tablecloths.

🔲 E6 ✉ 1215 Pine Street
☎ 206/621–7941 🕐 Dinner Mon–Sat

### PERFECT PIZZA

### MAD PIZZA ($)
Some of the city's best pizza at two locations.
In Fremont
✉ N 36th Avenue (west of Fremont Avenue N)
☎ 206/632–5453
In Madison Park
✉ 4021 E Madison
☎ 206/329–7037

### PAGLIACCI PIZZA ($)
Distinctive pizza, with choice of tradtional toppings or offbeat ones. At three locations.
In the University District
✉ 4529 University Way NE
☎ 206/726–1717
On Capitol Hill
✉ 426 Broadway E
☎ 206/324–0730
On Queen Anne
✉ 550 Queen Anne Avenue N
☎ 206/285–1232

### PEGASUS PIZZA ($)
Greek-style pizza that some consider Seattle's best.
In West Seattle.
✉ 2758 Alki Avenue SW
☎ 206/932–4849

# Romantic/Bistro Dining

### ANDALUCA ($$)

The freshest Northwest ingredients combine with the flavors of the Mediterranean to create a memorable culinary experience.

✚ E5 ✉ Mayflower Park Hotel, 405 Olive Way ☎ 206/382–6999 ⏰ Lunch and dinner daily

### CAFÉ CAMPAGNE ($$)

Dim and warm, this cozy spot in the Pike Place Market is perfect for a glass of wine. Sunday brunch is one of the best.

✚ F5 ✉ 1600 Post Alley ☎ 206/728–2233 ⏰ Lunch, and dinner daily, brunch on weekends

### CAFÉ NOLA ($$)

Hop on a ferry to Bainbridge Island and escape to the tidy tidings of this eclectic eatery.

✚ Off map ✉ 101 Winslow Way, Bainbridge Island ☎ 206/842–3822 ⏰ Lunch Mon–Fri, dinner nightly, brunch on weekends

### CASSIS ($$$)

Warm, inviting and intimate, this French bistro offers satisfying fare to flocks of loyal patrons.

✚ B4 ✉ 2359 10th Avenue E ☎ 206/329–0580 ⏰ Dinner nightly

### CHEZ SHEA ($$$)

An outstanding view from this delightful bistro with flower-topped white-linen tables makes for romance.

✚ F5 ✉ 94 Pike Street ☎ 206/467–9990 ⏰ Dinner Tue–Sun

### LA FONTANA ($$)

An urban romantic oasis filled with candlelight, and named for the fountain in the courtyard.

✚ E5 ✉ 120 Blanchard Street ☎ 206/441–1045 ⏰ Dinner nightly

### LE PICHET ($$)

*Café au lait* in the morning, baguettes at lunch and charcuterie and ever-changing specials at night make for casual French café dining at its best.

✚ E5 ✉ 1933 1st Avenue ☎ 206/256–1499 ⏰ Breakfast daily, lunch and dinner Thu–Sun

### LUSH LIFE ($$)

It's easy to walk right by this hidden Italian spot without noticing, but it's a true find for a romantic dinner or drink. Mostly traditional dishes served.

✚ E5 ✉ 2331 2nd Avenue ☎ 206/441–9842 ⏰ Dinner Mon–Sat

### MISTRAL ($$$)

Exquisite prix-fixe dining in a quiet respite in the heart of bustling Belltown.

✚ E5 ✉ 113 Blanchard Street ☎ 206/770–7799 ⏰ Lunch Sat–Sun, dinner Tue–Sat

### SERAFINA ($$)

Rustic Italian by candle-light and an outdoor deck to enjoy a summer evening.

✚ B4 ✉ 2043 Eastlake Avenue E ☎ 206/323–0807 ⏰ Lunch Mon–Fri, dinner nightly

### STELLA'S TRATTORIA ($)

In the University district, this 24-hour haunt serves late-night snacks with an Italian accent and break-fast the morning after.

✚ A6 ✉ 4500 9th Avenue N ☎ 206/633–1100 ⏰ 24 hours

# Coffee Shops & Breakfast Bests

### BAUHAUS ($)
Stylish coffee bar and bookstore offering choice people-watching and selling Ding Dongs.
✚ E6 ✉ 301 E Pine Street
☎ 206/625–1600
🕒 Mon–Fri 6am–1am, Sat, Sun 8–1

### B & O ESPRESSO ($)
Coffee and a wide selection of desserts in one of Seattle's classic espresso bars.
✚ D4 ✉ 204 Belmont Avenue E ☎ 206/322–5028
🕒 Daily 8am–midnight

### CAFÉ SEPTIEME ($)
Coffee and other diversions served with attitude to hipsters on Broadway.
✚ D4 ✉ 214 Broadway E
☎ 206/860–8858 🕒 Daily 9am–midnight (Fri, Sat till 2am )

### CAFFE LADRO ($)
Adirondack chairs line the front of these friendly neighborhood coffee shops. Two locations.
✚ A3; C5 ✉ 2205 Queen Anne Avenue N; 15th Avenue E on N Capitol Hill ☎ 206/ 282–5313; 206/267–0551

### ESPRESSO VIVACE ($)
The best place to get a cup of coffee in the city, with umbrella-shaded tables that are perfect for people-watching.
✚ D4 ✉ 321 Broadway E
☎ 206/860–5869

### MACRINA BAKERY ($)
Freshly baked breads and pastries, and shots of espresso greet sleepy urbanites. Freshly prepared daily "special" sandwiches and soups continue to draw crowds as the day wears on.
✚ E5 ✉ 2408 1st Avenue
☎ 206/448–4032 🕒 Daily 11am–3pm

### PANAMA HOTEL TEA & COFFEE HOUSE ($)
This International District café serves up more than 20 varieties of tea: In a building that was once a Japanese bathhouse, a window in the floor provides a glimpse at its former history, including belongings left behind by Japanese-Americans who were rounded up and sent to internment camps during World War II.
✚ E4 ✉ 605 S Main Street
☎ 206/515–4000 🕒 Mon– Sat 8am–10pm, Sun 9am–8pm

### TEAHOUSE KUAN YIN ($)
A quiet respite from the bustle of the city offering every imaginable sort of tea.
✚ A3 ✉ 1911 N 45th Street
☎ 206/632–2055 🕒 Daily 10–11pm (Fri, Sat till midnight)

### UPTOWN ESPRESSO ($)
This neghborhood coffee shop makes a great place to sit and sup a perfect latte, or a cappuccino with boast-worthy foam.
✚ A3 ✉ 525 Queen Anne Avenue N ☎ 206/281–8669

### ZEITGEIST KUNST AND KAFFEE ($)
Fresh espresso, inviting ambience, art displays and high-speed Internet access make this Pioneer Square café a popular haunt.
✚ E4 ✉ 171 S Jackson Street
☎ 206/583–0497 🕒 Daily 7am–7pm

## BAGELS

### BAGEL OASIS ($)
Delicious bagels with a variety of spreads. Several locations.
✚ A2 ✉ 462 N 36th Street, Fremont 🚌 26, 28
✚ F6 ✉ 4th and Seneca Streets 🕒 Lunch only

### SEATTLE BAGEL BAKERY ($)
First-rate bagels. Order "to go" for a picnic outside, on the Harbor Steps.
✚ F5 ✉ 1302 Western Avenue ☎ 206/624–2187

71

# Men's & Women's Clothing

## SHOPPING DISTRICTS

Seattle's finest clothing stores tend to be clustered in several neighborhoods. The Downtown retail core between Stewart and Pike (N–S) and 3rd and 6th Avenues includes Bon Marche (3rd and Pine), Nordstrom's (5th and Pine), City Center (1420 5th Avenue), Westlake Mall (4th and Pine). Nearby is Rainier Square (bounded by 4th and 5th Avenues and University–Union streets). Other areas include Belltown (1st and 2nd from Bell Street), Broadway East on Capitol Hill.

## DOWNTOWN CITY CENTER

### ALHAMBRA
Sophisticated clothing from dainty silk dresses to velvet yoga pants for women. Live jazz Saturday afternoons entertains while you shop.
✚ E6 ✉ 101 Pine Street
☎ 206/621–9571
🕐 Mon–Sat 10–6.30, Sun 11.30–6

### ANN TAYLOR
Classic lines and easy elegance in women's fashions ranging from career to informal wear.
✚ E3 ✉ 1420 5th Avenue
☎ 206/623–4818
🕐 Mon–Sat 10–7, Sun noon–6

### APRIL CORNELL
Feminine styles and charming, colorful prints for women.
✚ D3 ✉ Westlake Center
☎ 206/749–9658
🕐 Mon–Sat 9.30–8, Sun 11–6

### BARNEYS
Chic and trendy for that minimalist New York style. Prada and other popular designers.
✚ F6 ✉ 1420 5th Avenue
☎ 206/622–6300
🕐 Mon–Sat 10–6, Sun noon–5

### BCBG
Beautiful evening gowns, career and casual creations by Paris designer Max Azria.
✚ E6 ✉ 600 Pine Street
☎ 206/447–3400
🕐 Mon–Sat 9.30–8, Sun 11–6

### BETSEY JOHNSON
For adventuresome and young-at-heart women who like fun and flamboyance in their clothing.
✚ F6 ✉ 1429 5th Avenue
☎ 206/624–2887
🕐 Mon–Sat 11–7, Sun 11–6

### BROOKS BROTHERS
Superior men's clothing in traditional styles.
✚ F6 ✉ 1335 5th Avenue
☎ 206/624–4400
🕐 Mon–Fri 9.30–7, Sat 10–6, Sun noon–5

### BUTCH BLUM
Expensive European-styled men's apparel from famous designers' exclusive collections, as well as more original, avant-garde lines.
✚ F6 ✉ 1408 5th Avenue
☎ 206/524–5860
🕐 Mon–Sat 10–6, Sun noon–5

### CHICOS
Distinctive and fun women's clothes with attitude that travel easily. Mostly wash and wear.
✚ E6 ✉ 600 Pine Street
☎ 206/729–7099
🕐 Mon–Sat 9.30–8, Sun 11–6

### DAVID LAWRENCE
Stylish European men's fashion from suits to sportswear—Donna Karan, Hugo Boss, Versace.
✚ D3 ✉ 4th Avenue at Union
☎ 206/622–2544
🕐 Mon–Sat 10–7, Sun noon–5

### EARTH, WIND & FIRE
Women's boutique featuring stylish, handmade apparel including outer-wear for braving the weather with flair.
✚ F5 ✉ 1514 Pike Place #13
☎ 206/383–2153 or 206/448–2529 🕐 Daily 10–6

### EDDIE BAUER
Casual wear and accessories for men and women with

an outdoor lifestyle.

F6 ✉ 1330 5th Avenue
☎ 206/527–2646
🕐 Mon–Sat 10–8, Sun 11–6

### EILEEN FISHER
Simple yet elegant apparel
for the professional
woman of 30 or 65.

E6 ✉ 525 Pine Street
☎ 206/748–0770
🕐 Mon–Sat 10–7, Sun noon–5

### J. CREW
Stylish, casual wear for
men and women with the
emphasis on natural fibers
and comfort.

E6 ✉ 600 Pine Street
☎ 206/652–9788
🕐 Mon–Sat 9.30–8, Sun 11–6

### KENNETH COLE
This prominent designer
opened here in 2000,
featuring chic styles for
today's men and women.

E5 ✉ 520 Pike Street
☎ 206/382–1680
🕐 Mon–Sat 10–8, Sun noon–6

### MARIO'S
Fashionable downtown
store specializing in clean,
classic lines and featuring
designers like Donna
Karan and Giorgio Armani.

E6 ✉ 1513 6th Avenue
☎ 206/223–1461
🕐 Mon–Sat 10–6, Sun noon–5

### NORDSTROM
This venerable institution
stocks clothing and shoes
for the entire family.

E5 ✉ 500 Pine Street
☎ 206/628–2111
🕐 Mon–Sat 9.30–8, Sun 11–7

### NUBIAS
Relaxed sophistication for
women in styles that
reflect owner-designer
Nubia's Latin roots with

accents from Asia.

E6 ✉ 1306 4th Avenue
☎ 206/325–4854
🕐 Mon–Sat 10–6 ☐ 11

### PATAGONIA
State-of-the-art outdoor
clothing for adults and
children.

E5 ✉ 2100 1st Avenue
☎ 206/622–9700
🕐 Mon–Sat 10–6, Sun 11–5

### TOTALLY MICHAEL'S
Sophisticated women's
clothing for work, play
and after dark.

F6 ✉ 521 Union Street
☎ 206/622–4920
🕐 Mon–Sat 10–6

## BELLTOWN (ALONG 1ST AVENUE)

### BABY & CO.
Pricey, whimsical clothes
for adventurous women.

E5 ✉ 1936 1st Avenue
☎ 206/448–4077
🕐 Mon–Sat 10–6, Sun noon–5

### DARBURY STENDERU
Stunning wearable art for
women with hand-painted
designs; beautiful colors
and fabrics.

E5 ✉ 2121 1st Avenue
☎ 206/448–2625
🕐 Tue–Sat noon–6

### DITA BOUTIQUE
Unusual selections of
women's wear for all ages;
including many imports.

F5 ✉ 1525 1st Avenue, #2
☎ 206/622–1770
🕐 Mon–Sat 10–6, Sun noon–5

### ENDLESS KNOT
Elegant and original
women's clothes.

E5 ✉ 2300 1st Avenue
☎ 206/448–0355
🕐 Mon–Sat 11–6, Sun noon–5

### SEATTLE AREA SHOPPING MALLS

Bellevue Square
This suburban mall on the east
side of Lake has a vast array of
high-end clothing and
specialty shops, department
stores and eateries.

✉ NE 8th Street and Bellevue
Way NE 🕐 Mon–Sat
9.30–9.30, Sun 11–7
🚌 Downtown to Eastside
over SR520 floating bridge

University Village
With an upscale renovation
begining in 1995, U Village
now includes branches of a
number of major players in
the retail market.

✉ NE 45th and 25th Avenue
NE, east of the University of
Washington campus
🕐 Mon–Sat 9.30–9, Sun 11–6
🚌 From downtown

Northgate Mall
The first enclosed mall in the
United States, Northgate
opened in 1950. Renovated in
the late 1990's, the mall
includes four department
stores, an assortment of small
stores and a food court.

✉ I5 north to 110th NE
(Northgate Way) 🕐 Mon–Sat
10–9.30, Sun 11–6 🚌 Express
service from downtown to
Northgate station

## SIZE CONVERSION

A = America
B = Britain
F = France
I = Italy
E = Rest of Europe

### Women's clothes

| A | 8 | 10 | 12 | 14 | 16 |
|---|---|----|----|----|----|
| B | 10 | 12 | 14 | 16 | 18 |
| F | 38 | 40 | 42 | 46 | 48 |
| I | 40 | 42 | 44 | 46 | 48 |
| E | 36 | 38 | 40 | 42 | 44 |

### Men's shirts

| A | 14½ | 15 | 15½ | 16 | 16½ |
|---|-----|----|-----|----|-----|
| B | 14½ | 15 | 15½ | 16 | 16½ |
| E | 37 | 38 | 39/40 | 41 | 42 |

### Shoes

| A | 5½ | 6½ | 7½ | 8½ | 9½ | 10½ | 11½ |
|---|----|----|----|----|----|-----|-----|
| B | 4 | 5 | 6 | 7 | 8 | 9 | 11 |
| E | 36 | 38 | 39 | 40 | 41 | 42 | 44 |

## OPUS 204

Custom designed women's clothing, jewelry and accessories—simple, yet sophisticated lines in beautiful fabrics. Antiques and collectibles as well.
✚ E5 ⊠ 2004 1st Avenue ☎ 206/728–7707 🕐 Mon–Sat 10–6, Sun noon–5 🚇 7

## TULIP

This new addition to Seattle's high fashion scene carries the lines of small, exclusive designers such as Miguelina and Joie Tocca with an emphasis on "feminine and girly."
✚ F5 ⊠ 1201 1st Avenue ☎ 206/223–1790 🕐 Mon–Sat 9.30–9, Sun 11–6

## CAPITOL HILL

### REI

Outdoor clothing and gear runs the gamut from hiking equipment to bikes, kayaks and books.
✚ D4 ⊠ 222 Yale Avenue N ☎ 206/223–1944 🕐 Mon–Fri 10–9, Sat–Sun 10–7

### URBAN OUTFITTERS

New and vintage clothing popular with the young and trendy; also sells housewares, jewelry and gifts. In Broadway Market.
✚ D4 ⊠ 401 Broadway E ☎ 206/381–3777 🕐 Mon–Sat 10–8, Sun 11–7 🚇 7

### YAZDI'S

Dresses, skirts, vests, and softly draping pants for women—made of rayon and cotton in beautiful Indonesian prints.
✚ D4 ⊠ 401 Broadway E ☎ 206/860–7109 🕐 Mon–Sat 10–8, Sun noon–6 🚇 7

## PIONEER SQUARE

### FILSON RETAIL STORE

This century-old company has provided clothing and gear for outdoorsmen since before the Alaska Gold Rush. Their natural fiber apparel is favored by those seeking rugged, all-weather gear made-to-last. You can watch as the merchandise is patterned and assembled in the on-site workshop.
✚ F4 ⊠ 1555 4th Avenue S ☎ 206/622–3147 🕐 Mon–Sat 10–7, Sun 10–5

### RAGAZZI'S FLYING SHUTTLE

Eye-catching hand-woven women's clothing and wearable art; handpainted silk purses and scarves complemented by the exquisite jewelry.
✚ G6 ⊠ 607 1st Avenue ☎ 206/343–9762 🕐 Mon–Sat 10.30–5.30

## UNIVERSITY VILLAGE

### ABERCROMBIE & FITCH

Well-made clothes for well-heeled men and women.
✚ A6 ⊠ 2540 NE University Village ☎ 206/729–3510 🕐 Mon–Sat 9.30–9, Sun 11–6

### BRYN WALKER

Comfy, casual clothes for women made of natural fibers reign at this fun boutique.
✚ A6 ⊠ Corner of NE 45th Street and 25th Avenue NE ☎ 206/525–0698 🕐 Mon–Sat 9.30–9, Sun 11–6

# Art & Antiques

### AZUMA GALLERY
Japanese art including old and new prints, paintings, screens, folk art and ceramics.
+ G6 ✉ 530 1st Avenue S
☎ 206/622–5599
🕒 Tue–Sat 11–6

### FLURY & CO. GALLERY
Vintage photographs of Native American life; Native American artifacts, beadwork and carvings.
+ F3 ✉ 322 1st Avenue S
☎ 206/587–0260
🕒 Mon–Sat 10–6

### FOSTER-WHITE GALLERY
Work by Pilchuk Glass artists like Dale Chihuly and other prominent artists.
+ G6 ✉ 123 S Jackson
☎ 206/622–2833 🕒 Mon–Sat 10–5.30, Sun noon–5

### FRANCINE SEDERS GALLERY
In addition to famous names like Jacob Lawrence and Michael Spafford, Seders represents a growing number of minority artists.
+ Off map ✉ 6701 Greenwood Avenue N (west of Green Lake) ☎ 206/782–0355 🕒 Tue–Sat 11–5, Sun 1–5

### G. GIBSON GALLERY
Photographs and related fine art including works by notable Northwest artists like Marsha Burns.
+ D4 ✉ 514 Pike Street (on Capitol Hill) ☎ 206/587–4033 🕒 Wed–Fri 11–6, Sat 11–5

### GREG KUCERA GALLERY
A top city gallery.
+ G6 ✉ 212 3rd Avenue S
☎ 206/624–0770 🕒 Tue–Sat 10.30–5.30, Sun 1–5

### HONEYCHURCH ANTIQUES
The foremost store for fine Asian antiques, especially Japanese and Chinese.
+ E4 ✉ 1008 James Street
☎ 206/622–1225
🕒 Mon–Sat 10–6

### THE LEGACY
Seattle's oldest and finest gallery for Northwest Native American and Inuit art and artifacts. Founded in 1933.
+ G6 ✉ 1003 1st Avenue
☎ 206/624–6350
🕒 Mon–Sat 10–6

### NORTHWEST GALLERY OF FINE WOODWORKING
Local artists' cooperative that exhibits phenomenal craftsmanship and design.
+ G6 ✉ 101 S Jackson
☎ 206/625–0542 🕒 Mon–Sat 10.30–5.30, Sun noon–5

### STONINGTON GALLERY
Works by native Northwest Coast master artists Joe David, Robert Davidson, Bill Holm, Duane Pasco and by owner Nancy Stonington.
+ E5 ✉ 119 S Jackson
☎ 206/405–4040,
www.stoningtongallery.com
🕒 Mon–Fri 10–6, Sat 10–5.30, Sun noon–5

### WILLIAM TRAVER GALLERY
Contemporary painting, sculpture and ceramics by major artists. The gallery is also a leading dealer in contemporary studio glass.
+ F5 ✉ 110 Union, 2nd floor
☎ 206/587–6501;
www.travergallery.com
🕒 Mon–Fri 10–6, Sat 10–5, Sun noon–5

### ART AND ANTIQUES

### FIRST THURSDAY GALLERY WALKS
On the first Thursday of the month, Pioneer Square galleries and those in the Pike Market area open into the evening for the monthly art walk. Many galleries take this opportunity to preview their new shows.

### THE PILCHUCK SCHOOL
The Seattle area is well-known for its glass art, primarily through the work of Dale Chihuly and others connected to the world-class Pilchuck Glass School, 50 miles (81km) north of Seattle. Examples of Chihuly's work include the large, entry-wall chandeliers at Benaroye Hall and several pieces on display at City Center shopping arcade.

# Books, CDs & Tapes

## THE INDEPENDENT BOOKSELLER

Seattle has a number of excellent independent booksellers who are committed to bringing quality literature to the public, both blockbusters and smaller works appealing to a more specialized audience. With the arrival of national chains and their well-appointed superstores, independents are feeling the pinch.

## ALL FOR KIDS BOOKS AND MUSIC

A wide selection of children's books, music and books-on-tape.
➕ Off map ✉ 2900 NE Blakely Street (by University Village) ☎ 206/526–2768 🚌 25 🕐 Mon–Sat 10–6, Sun noon–5

## BAILEY-COY BOOKS

Well-stocked bookstore with a good selection of gay and lesbian titles.
➕ D4 ✉ 414 Broadway E ☎ 206/323–8842 🕐 Mon–Sat 10–10, Sun 10–9 🚌 7

## EAST-WEST BOOKSHOP

One of the region's largest stocks of New Age books.
➕ A6 ✉ 1032 NE 65th Street ☎ 206/523–3726 🕐 Mon–Sat 10–9, Sun noon–6.30 🚌 48, 66

## ELLIOTT BAY BOOK COMPANY

More than 130,000 titles, frequent readings and a café in this Pioneer Square haunt.
➕ G6 ✉ 101 S Main Street ☎ 206/624–6600 🕐 Mon–Sat 9.30–10, Sun 11–7

## FREMONT PLACE BOOK COMPANY

This small, cheerful shop features contemporary fiction, Northwest authors, gay and lesbian literature and children's books.
➕ A2 ✉ 621 N 35th Street ☎ 206/547–5970 🕐 Mon–Sat 10–8, Sun noon–6

## SECOND STORY BOOKS

Small store on the upper floor of Wallingford Center with an excellent choice of titles.
➕ Off map ✉ 1815 N 45th ☎ 206/547–4605 🕐 Mon–Sat 10–8, Sat 11–6, Sun 11–5 🚌 16

## SILVER PLATTERS

With its huge selection of over 6,000 CDs, this is *the* place to locate that hard-to-find title.
➕ A4 ✉ 9650 1st Avenue NE (near Northgate Mall) ☎ 206/524–3472; www.silverplatters.com 🕐 Mon–Sat 10–10, Sun 11–7

## TOWER RECORDS

An awesome variety of music for every taste. An in-store Ticketmaster sells tickets to concerts.
➕ A6 ✉ 4321 University Way NE ☎ 206/632–1187 🕐 Daily 10–10 🚌 71, 72, 73, 43

## TWICE-SOLD TALES

Wonderful secondhand bookstore.
➕ D4 ✉ 905 E John Street ☎ 206/324–2421 🕐 Sun–Thu 10–midnight, Fri open 24 hours, Sat 10–2am 🚌 7, 43

## UNIVERSITY BOOKSTORE

One of the nation's largest university bookstores. Also sells art and office supplies, gifts and CDs.
➕ D5 ✉ 4326 University Way NE ☎ 206/634–3400 🕐 Mon–Sat 9–9, Sun noon–5 🚌 71, 72, 73, 43

## WIDE WORLD BOOKS & MAPS

Everything you'll need to plan your travels. Wallingford area.
➕ A3 ✉ 4411 Wallingford Avenue N ☎ 206/634–3453 🕐 Mon–Sat 10–9, Sun 10–7

# Gifts

### CALDWELL'S

Wonderful imports like folk art, textiles and jewelry from Central and South America, Africa and Asia.

➕ A6 ✉ 2646 University Village NE ☎ 206/522–7531 🕐 Mon–Sat 9.30–9, Sun 11–6 🚌 25

### CRACKERJACK CONTEMPORARY CRAFTS

Unique handcrafted items —many by local artists.

➕ Off map ✉ 1815 N 45th Street (Wallingford Center) ☎ 206/547–4983 🕐 Mon–Sat 10–8, Sun 11–5 🚌 16

### DESIGN CONCERN

First-rate design in everything from desk accessories and housewares to jewelry.

➕ F6 ✉ 1420 5th Avenue (City Center) ☎ 206/623–4444 🕐 Mon–Sat 10–6, Sun noon–5

### FIREWORKS FINE CRAFTS GALLERY

Where crafts meet art, for the playful, the beautiful and unique. Three locations.

➕ G6 ✉ 210 1st Avenue S ☎ 206/682–8707
➕ E6 ✉ Westlake Center ☎ 206/682–6462
➕ A6 ✉ University Village Mall ☎ 206/527–2858 🕐 Mon–Sat 9.30–9, Sun 11–6

### FOUND OBJECTS

One-of-a-kind artifacts from the quirky—like a mahogany and ivory gun powder measuring stick— to unusual artist-made jewelry and furnishings.

➕ F5 ✉ 1406 1st Avenue ☎ 206/682–4324 🕐 Mon–Sat 10–6, Sun noon–5

### KOBO

Objects with a distinctive Japanese flavor.

➕ C3 ✉ 814 E Roy Street on Capitol Hill ☎ 206/726–0704 🕐 Daily noon–7

### LA TIENDA FOLK ART GALLERY

Handcrafted folk art, textiles, women's apparel, jewelry and musical instruments.

➕ A6 ✉ 4138 University Way NE ☎ 206/632–1796 🕐 Mon–Sat 10–6 🚌 71, 72, 73, 43

### MADE IN WASHINGTON

Handcrafts, foods and wines from the region. Shipping available.

➕ E6 ✉ 400 Pine Street, suite 114, Westlake Center ☎ 206/623–9753 🕐 Mon–Sat 10–8, Sun 11–6

### PHOENIX RISING GALLERY

Fine crafts gallery in the north end of the Market showcasing beautiful and original jewelry, ceramics, and glassware.

➕ F5 ✉ 2030 Western Avenue in the Pike Place Market ☎ 206/728–2332 🕐 Daily 10–6

### PORTAGE BAY GOODS

Environmentally friendly gifts by local and worldwide artisans.

➕ B3 ✉ 706 N 34th ☎ 206/547–5221 🕐 Mon–Sat 10–7, Sun 10–6

### UZURI

A potpourri of ethnic gifts, many from Africa, including jewelry, carvings, baskets and clothing.

➕ D4 ✉ 401 Broadway East (in the Broadway Market) ☎ 206/323–3238 🕐 Mon–Thu 10–9, Fri–Sat 10–10, Sun noon–6

### TASTES OF SEATTLE

What better way to elicit the flavor of the region than to take back a salmon and a bottle of Washington wine. Fishsellers at the Pike Place Market will pack fresh salmon on ice to travel and many fish markets and gift stores like "Made in Washington" carry gift boxes of smoked salmon that do not require refrigeration.

# Specialty Shops

## UWAJIMAYA

In 1928, Fujimatsu Moriguchi began a small business in Tacoma, Washington selling fish cakes from the back of his truck to Japanese loggers and fishermen. He named the business after the Japanese town where he had learned his trade. After World War II, the family moved to Seattle and opened their first retail store in Seattle's international district. Today, Uwajimaya is the largest gift and grocery store in the Pacific Northwest. A new Uwajimaya Village opened in late 2000, one block south of its former site. The expanded emporium includes several other on-site businesses including Kinokuniya Bookstore, the largest Japanese bookstore chain in the United States, and an Asian food court. Cooking classes offered.
✉ 5th Avenue S at Dearborn
☎ 206/624-6248

## FACERE JEWELRY ART

One-of-a-kind Victorian and contemporary jewelry.
✚ F6 ✉ 1420 5th Avenue in City Center ☎ 206/624-6768
⏰ Mon–Sat 10–6

## FOX'S GEM SHOP

Fine jewelry since 1912. Expensive.
✚ F6 ✉ 1341 5th Avenue
☎ 206/623-2528
⏰ Mon–Sat 10–6

## FRANK AND DUNYA

Fun, functional and fine arts and crafts by local artists.
✚ A3 ✉ 3418 Fremont Avenue N ☎ 206/547-6760
⏰ Sun–Thu 10–6, Fri–Sat 10–7

## IMPRESS RUBBER STAMPS

Thousands of rubber stamps, pads and papers.
✚ E6 ✉ 400 Pine Street in Westlake Center
☎ 206/621-1878 ⏰ Sun–Fri 7.30–8, Sun 11–5

## LARK IN THE MORNING

Beautiful handmade musical instruments. In Pike Place Market.
✚ E5 ✉ 1411 1st Avenue
☎ 206/623-3440
⏰ Mon–Sat 10–6, Sun noon–5

## MAGIC MOUSE

Fanciful, high-end toys for kids of all ages.
✚ E5 ✉ 603 1st Avenue
☎ 206/682-8097
⏰ Mon–Thu, Sun 10–6, Fri–Sat 10–9

## MARKET MAGIC SHOP

Supplies for budding young magicians to pros.
✚ F5 ✉ 1st level below the food stalls, Pike Place Market
☎ 206/624-4271
⏰ Mon–Sat 9.30–6, Sun 10–5

## METZKER MAPS

A wonderful selection of maps of the region and the rest of the world.
✚ E5 ✉ 702 1st Avenue
☎ 206/623-8747
⏰ Mon–Fri 9–6, Sat 10–5

## THE SHARPER IMAGE

State-of-the-art gadgets.
✚ E6 ✉ 1501 4th Avenue, Suite 116 ☎ 206/343-9125
⏰ Mon–Sat 10–6, Sun 11–5

## SOMETHING SILVER

All manner of jewelry, charms and key-chains made of sterling silver.
✚ A6 ✉ 2662 NE University Village ☎ 206/523-7545
⏰ Mon–Sat 11–9, Sun 11–6

## THREE DOG BAKERY

Items for that precious pooch, from a vest-style carrier for small pets to "bark and fetch" biscuits in apple cinnamon, barbeque, peanut butter and carob chip flavors.
✚ E5 ✉ 1408 1st Avenue
☎ 206/364-9999
⏰ Mon–Sat 10–6, Sun noon–5

## TRAVELERS

An unusual collection of items from jewelry and textiles, to Shiva lunchboxes and incense.
✚ E5 ✉ 501 E Pine Street
☎ 206/329-6260 ⏰ Sun–Thu 10–8, Fri–Sat 10–10

## YE OLDE CURIOSITY SHOP

Century-old store cum museum with a fascinating mix of Northwest momentos—many bizarre or grotesque.
✚ G5 ✉ Pier 54 on Alaskan Way ☎ 206/682-5844
⏰ Mon–Thu 10–6, Fri–Sat 9–9, Sun 9.30–6

# Kitsch, Funk & Retro

### ARCHIE McPHEE & CO.

First stop for gag gifts and novelties including plastic cockroaches, inflatable sharks, rubber chickens and boxing nun puppets.

✚ A3 ✉ 2428 NW Market Street ☎ 206/297–0240 🚌 17, 18 🕐 Mon–Sat 9–7, Sun 10–6

### BUFFALO EXCHANGE

This popular University District consignment store carries all manner of clothes, accessories, shoes and wigs.

✚ A6 ✉ 4530 University Way NE ☎ 206/545–0175 🚌 71, 72, 73, 43 🕐 Mon–Sat 11–8, Sun 11–7

### DELUXE JUNK

This offbeat store in Seattle's Fremont neighborhood has been a local icon for years. The name says it all!

✚ A3 ✉ 3518 Fremont Place N 🕐 Mon, Wed, Fri, Sat, Sun 11–5.30

### FREMONT ANTIQUE MALL

Fifty different dealers share this rambling space in Fremont and sell everything from clothes, antiques and collectibles to records and toys. Visit the Macabre Corner for strange items like a William Burroughs' finger painting and Ed "Big Daddy" Roth memorabilia.

✚ A2 ✉ 3419 Fremont Place N ☎ 206/548–9140 🕐 Mon–Fri 11–7, Sat–Sun 10–7

### FRITZI RITZ

Men's and women's vintage clothing, hats, shoes and wigs, labeled by decade.

✚ A2 ✉ 750 N 34th Street, Fremont ☎ 206/633–0929 🕐 Tue–Fri noon–6, Sat noon–5.30, Sun noon–5

### ISADORAS

High-end vintage finery: beaded cocktail dresses, vintage gowns and, for men, suits, hats and ties.

✚ E5 ✉ 1915 1st Avenue, 2 blocks north of Market ☎ 206/441–7711 🕐 Mon–Thu 11–6, Fri 11–8, Sat 10–6, Sun noon–5

### LE FROCK

Recycled and vintage clothing for both men and women. Also designer samples of both national and local designers like Ann Ferriday, Kate Spade, Prada and Versace.

✚ C5 ✉ 317 E Pine Street on Capitol Hill ☎ 206/623–5339 🕐 Mon–Sat 10–7, Sun 11–5

### RED LIGHT

Glitzy platform shoes, wigs, retro pants and tops.

✚ Off map ✉ 4560 University Way NE ☎ 206/545–4044 🕐 Mon–Fri 11–8, Sun 11–7 🚌 71, 72, 73, 43

### RETRO VIVA

Retro apparel and jewelry in the University District.

✚ A6 ✉ 4536 University Way NE ☎ 206/632–8886 🕐 Mon–Sat 11–7, Sun 11–6 🚌 71, 72, 73, 43

### RHINESTONE ROSIE

Estate and costume jewelry treasures, 1870–1970, restored and repaired. For sale or rent.

✚ B2 ✉ 606 W Crockett, Queen Anne ☎ 206/283–4605 🕐 Tue–Fri 11–5, or call for an appointment

### FREMONT FUNK

With *De Libertas Quirkas* (the right to be quirky) as its motto, it's no wonder that Seattle's Fremont neighborhood is both the birthplace and breeding ground of local funk. In the 1960s and 1970s artists, bohemians and students began moving into old brick buildings that had fallen into disrepair. Attracted by low rents, these new residents set up studios, shops and cafés that established a playful, down-home aesthetic. Before long, they'd formed the Fremont Arts Council charged with helping create a sense of community through art…and not the highbrow art of cultural institutions, but accessible art with a sense of humor. Their concept of art embraced both whimsical public sculptures like *Waiting for the Interurban*, and the *Fremont Troll* (➤ 55), and community festivals and events.

# Theater & Film

## TEATRO ZINZANNI

This high-spirited theatrical and culinary experience opened in the summer of 1998 in a temporary big-top adjacent to Seattle Center. Described as "the place where the Moulin Rouge meets Cirque du Soleil," the evening's entertainment included elements of cabaret, circus, magic and live music. After a wildly successful run, the producers moved their offbeat dinner theater to a permanent home—a former Cadillac dealership in Belltown—and transformed the space into an antique nightclub. Dinner features a five-course meal created by acclaimed Seattle chef, Tom Douglas.

✉ 2301 6th Avenue at Battery Street ☎ 206/802-0015; www.zinzanni.org ⏰ Doors open Wed–Sat at 6pm, Sun at 5pm 💲 Expensive
❓ Tickets at box office or by phone or website. Dress code no jeans or t-shirts

## FILM

Seattle is a great place for film buffs. The city hosts an annual International Film Festival in May and June that is the largest in the United States. Other festivals include Women in Cinema and Jewish, Irish and Asian festivals.

## THEATER

### A CONTEMPORARY THEATER (ACT)

Contemporary plays May–December; the season always closes with *A Christmas Carol*.
✚ C2 ✉ 700 Union Street ☎ 206/292-7676

### CREPE DE PARIS

Seattle's downtown dinner theater; French cuisine and cabaret. Terrace. Reservations recommended.
✚ F6 ✉ 1333 5th Avenue at Rainier Square ☎ 206/623-4111 ⏰ Mon–Sat

### THE EMPTY SPACE THEATER

Bold, imaginative theatrical presentations in funky Fremont.
✚ A3 ✉ 3509 Fremont Avenue N ☎ 206/547-7500 🚌 26

### FIFTH AVENUE THEATER

This historic, ornate hall hosts new productions of classic musicals and touring Broadway shows.
✚ F6 ✉ 1308 5th Avenue ☎ 206/625-1900

### INTIMAN THEATER

Pulitzer Prize-winning regional company that focuses on modern plays and the classics. Season runs May–December.
✚ C2 ✉ 201 Mercer Street, Seattle Center ☎ 206/269-1900 🚌 1, 2, 13

### PARAMOUNT THEATER

A lovingly restored 1920s movie palace that stages touring Broadway blockbusters.
✚ E6 ✉ 911 Pine Street ☎ 206/682-1414

## NORTHWEST ASIAN–AMERICAN THEATER

The Northwest's only Asian-American theater mounts productions in the International District.
✚ E4 ✉ 409 7th Avenue S at Jackson ☎ 206/340-1445

### SEATTLE REPERTORY THEATER

Seattle's oldest theater company, with two venues, presents updated classics, recent off-Broadway and regional plays and premiers of works by up-and-coming playwrights. Season runs October–May.
✚ C2 ✉ Bagley Wright Theater, Seattle Center ☎ 206/443-2222 🚌 1, 2, 13, 15, 18

## FILM HOUSES

### GUILD 45TH

Two neighboring theaters in the Wallingford district.
✚ A6 ✉ 2115 N 45th Street ☎ 206/633-3353

### THE EGYPTIAN

This former Masonic Temple features non-mainstream current releases.
✚ C5 ✉ 801 E Pine Street (Capitol Hill) ☎ 206/323-4978

### HARVARD EXIT

Consistently strong programing featuring off-beat current releases in an old Capitol Hill Mansion.
✚ C4 ✉ 807 E Roy ☎ 206/323-8986

### SEVEN GABLES

This cozy, converted residence in the University District features arthouse films.
✚ A6 ✉ 911 NE 50th Street ☎ 206/632-8820

# Classical Music, Dance & Opera

## CLASSICAL MUSIC

### FRYE MUSEUM CONCERT SERIES

The Ladies Musical Club presents free Sunday afternoon chamber music concerts at 2pm roughly once a month at the Frye.
🚩 E4 ✉ 704 Terry Avenue ☎ 206/622–9250 🚌 3, 4

### INTERNATIONAL CHAMBER MUSIC SERIES

Renowned chamber music ensembles perform from fall to spring as part of the University of Washington's "World Series at Meany Hall."
🚩 A5 ✉ Meany Theater, University of Washington, 4001 University Way NE ☎ 206/543–4880

### OLYMPIC MUSIC FESTIVAL

The Philadelphia String Quartet and other celebrated musicians perform in a turn-of-the-century barn on the Olympic Peninsula near Port Townsend, June–September.
🚩 A5 ☎ 206/527–8839

### SEATTLE CHAMBER MUSIC FESTIVAL

Popular summer series performances (July–August), with pre-concert dining on the lawns of the picturesque Lakeside School.
🚩 A4 ✉ Lakeside School, 14050 1st Avenue NE ☎ 206/283–8808 🚌 307 to Northgate, then 317

### SEATTLE SYMPHONY ORCHESTRA

A wide variety of classical music concerts September through mid-June held in Benaroya Hall.
🚩 C3 ✉ 2nd and University ☎ 206/215–4747

## DANCE

### MEANY HALL'S WORLD DANCE SERIES

This October–May series features ballet, modern and ethnic dance; Seattle native Mark Morris is a frequent presence.
🚩 A5 ✉ Meany Hall, University of Washington ☎ 206/543–4880

### ON THE BOARDS/ CENTER FOR CONTEMPORARY PERFORMANCE

Presentations integrate dance, theater, music and visual media.
🚩 C2 ✉ 100 West Roy ☎ 206/217–9888 🚌 15, 18

### PACIFIC NORTHWEST BALLET

Renowned company under the direction of former New York City Ballet dancers. The repertory mixes contemporary and classical, including rarely performed Balanchine ballets.
🚩 C3 ✉ Phelps Center, 301 Mercer Street, Seattle Center ☎ 206/441–9411 🚌 1, 2, 13

## OPERA

### SEATTLE OPERA

One of the nation's preeminent opera companies, with four or five full-scale productions September through May.
🚩 C3 ✉ Opera House, 321 Mercer Street, Seattle Center ☎ 206/389–7676 🚌 1, 2, 13

### TICKET/TICKET

Ticket sells remaining tickets for music, dance, theater, and comedy venues at half-price on the day of the show. Cash only, at two locations:
🚩 F5 ✉ Pike Place Market at the 1st and Pike Information booth 🕐 Every day except Mon, noon–6pm
🚩 D4 ✉ Broadway Market, second level, 401 Broadway E at E Harrison 🕐 Tue–Sat 10–7, Sun noon–6

### SEATTLE OUTDOOR CONCERT SERIES

In summer, Seattleites enjoy several outdoor concert series including:
• Out-to-Lunch noontime "brown bag" concerts at various downtown locations.
• Wednesday evening folk and pop concerts at the Woodland Park zoo bandshell.
• Summer Nights at the Pier, a waterfront concert series featuring big-name performers of pop, rock, R&B and blues. Third week of June through late August.
🚩 F5 ✉ Pier 62/63 by the Aquarium ☎ Hotline 206/281–8111; www.onereel.org

# Rock, Jazz & Blues Venues

## JOINT COVER

A number of Pioneer Square Blues and Jazz Clubs offer a joint cover for club-hopping. They include Bohemian Café, Central Saloon, Larry's, the Old Timers Café, the Fenix and The New Orleans.

## WHITE RIVER AMPHITHEATRE

This state-of-the-art outdoor concert venue, with an audience capacity of 20,000, opened in June 2003 after a protracted legal battle. Built to accommodate big-name rock stars and bands that can draw large crowds, the White River Amphitheatre boasts stunning views of Mt. Rainer. Owned by the tribe and located 35 miles (56km) south of Seattle on the Muckleshoot Indian Reservation, the amphitheater is sculpted from the earth, with 8,500 of its seats under a roof that extends from the stage. The rest of the audience sits on a grassy lawn. Two giant video screens bring performers up close. The tribe plans to offer 30 to 40 concerts during the summer season each year.

✉ 40601 Auburn-Enumclaw Road, Auburn
☎ 206/494–2134; www. whiteriveramphitheatre.com

## BALTIC ROOM

This elegant, trendy lounge features live music—mostly piano jazz, stiff drinks and a Wednesday "jungle night." Dancing, too.
✚ E6 ✉ 1207 Pine Street ☎ 206/625–4444

## CONOR-BYRNE'S PUBLIC HOUSE

This traditional Irish pub features live bands Thursday through Saturday, an Irish jam session Sundays at 9 and set dancing on a regular basis.
✚ Off map ✉ 5140 Ballard Avenue NW ☎ 206/784–3640; www.conorspub.com

## CROCODILE

Hippest local and national touring bands play here at this birthplace of grunge, still co-owned by wife of REM guitarist Peter Buck.
✚ E5 ✉ 2200 2nd Avenue ☎ 206/441–5611

## DIMITRIOU'S JAZZ ALLEY

Legendary jazz performers in a pleasant setting. Dinner before ensures a good seat.
✚ D3 ✉ 2033 Sixth Avenue ☎ 206/441–9729; www.jazzalley.com

## EL GAUCHO PAMPAS ROOM

Jazz supper club open Friday and Saturday nights. Round tables, understated lighting, a large dance floor and a large stage. Cabaret-style entertainment. Latin jazz and world music.
✚ D3 ✉ 72505 1st Avenue ☎ 206/728–1140

## FENIX

A new "Fenix" rose from the rubble after earthquake damage destroyed the club in its former incarnation. Live music ranging from rock to world music.
✚ G6 ✉ 101 S Washington Street ☎ 206/405–4323; www.fenixunderground.com

## GRATEFUL BREAD CAFÉ

This soup and sandwich bakery by day turns into an acoustic folk club by night. Seattle Folklore Society maintains the schedule.
✚ Off map ✉ 7001 35th Avenue NE ☎ 206/525–3166 (café); 206/782–0505 (folk club)

## LARRY'S BLUES CLUB

Blues, R&B and burgers in Pioneer Square.
✚ G6 ✉ 209 1st Avenue S ☎ 206/624–7665

## NEW ORLEANS CREOLE RESTAURANT

Cajun zydeco and jazz in Pioneer Square.
✚ G6 ✉ 114 1st Avenue S ☎ 206/622–2563

## PARAMOUNT THEATER

Seattle's premiere main-stage for the concert tours of superstars and for traveling musical theater productions. Built in 1928 as a silent film and vaudeville house, it has been beautifully restored to its former grandeur.
✚ E6 ✉ 911 Pine Street ☎ 206/682–1414; www.paramount.com

## TRACTOR TAVERN

A popular spot featuring live shows 5–7 nights a week—rock, Celtic, Cajun, bluegrass and country.
✚ G2 ✉ 5213 Ballard Avenue NW ☎ 206/789–3599; www.tractortavern.com

# Other Venues & Hangouts

## BELLTOWN BILLIARDS

This high-class bar, pool hall and Italian restaurant presents live jazz on Sunday and Monday and a Chardonnay "happy hour" weekdays between 4–7pm with half-price pool.
➕ E5 ✉ 90 Blanchard ☎ 206/448–6779 🕐 Tue–Fri 11.30am–2am, Sat–Mon 4pm–2am

## COMEDY UNDERGROUND

National and local comedy acts with audience participation. Located under Swannie's Restaurant.
➕ G6 ✉ 222 S Main Street ☎ 206/628–0303; www.comedyunderground.com

## GIGGLES

Microbrews on tap, cheap eats and hit-and-miss comedy. College crowd. Thursdays and Sundays are open mike comic showcase nights. University District.
➕ A6 ✉ 5220 Roosevelt Way NE ☎ 206/526–5653 🚌 66

## GLOBE CAFE

Open-mike poetry on Sundays. Sunday spoken-word events have been produced by Red Sky Poetry for almost 20 years, making these the longest continuously running events of their kind on the West Coast.
➕ D5 ✉ 1531 14th Avenue ☎ 206/324–8815 🕐 Tue–Sun 7am–7pm

## JILLIAN'S BILLIARD CLUB & CAFE

Two floors of pool and a restaurant plus the original bar from New York's Algonquin Hotel.
➕ D3 ✉ 731 Westlake N ☎ 206/223–0300 🕐 Mon–Fri till 2am, Sat–Sun till 4am

## PACIFIC SCIENCE CENTER LASER SHOWS

Laser light shows to rock music Thursday to Sunday evenings.
➕ D2 ✉ 2nd N at Seattle Center ☎ 206/443–2850 🚌 1, 2,13, 15, 18, 24, 33

## RICHARD HUGO HOUSE

Seattle's welcoming literary arts gathering place. Frequent readings and other programing.
➕ D4 ✉ 1634 11th Avenue ☎ 206/322–7030

## TEMPLE BILLIARDS

Two floors of pool tables, food at reasonable prices, a full bar and a funky jukebox attracts an eclectic crowd, ranging from the young and hip to old-time regulars, to this tucked-away haunt.
➕ G6 ✉ 126 S Jackson Street ☎ 206/682–3242 🕐 Mon–Fri 11am–2am, Sat–Sun 3pm–2am

## THEATERSPORTS

Unexpected Productions presents improvisational drama evenings at the Market Theater.
➕ F5 ✉ 1428 Post Alley at the Pike Street Market ☎ 206/781–9273 🕐 Fri, Sat at 10pm, Sun at 7pm

## UNIVERSITY OF WASHINGTON OBSERVATORY

During bad weather see a slide show on astronomy. Free star-gazing Monday–Thursday 9–11pm.
➕ A6 ✉ Entrance to campus at NE 45th and 17th Avenue NE ☎ 206/543–0126

## SEATTLE AND THE SPOKEN WORD

Each year Seattle hosts a vast number and variety of literary events, from the distinguished Seattle Arts and Literature series running September through May in which some of the world's finest writers speak and read from their work. Other spoken word venues include Seattle's annual Poetry Festival held the last weekend in April through the first weekend in May.

## SEATTLE POETRY SLAMS

Every Wednesday at 8pm, local poets and wordsmiths gather at rotating locations around the city for the weekly poetry slam. Participants must abide by the four basic rules of the National Poetry Slam organization: no props; must be original material performed by its author; don't go over 3 minutes and check your ego at the door. Judges are chosen from the audience. For information ☎ 206/760–1550; www.poetryfestival.org

# Bars, Pubs & Taverns

## GAY SEATTLE

Seattle's liberal attitudes and acceptance of alternative lifestyles has attracted a sizable gay and lesbian population centered around Capitol Hill's Pike/Pine corridor. Tracing its roots to the 1930s, the population increased after 1946 when gay servicemen stationed nearby moved to the city. In 1969, Dorian House was established "to provide counseling and employment help to homosexuals in the Seattle area." It was the first organization of its kind in the United States. Some five years later, Seattle held a Gay Pride celebration featuring a parade down Broadway followed by a rally at Volunteer Park. While the first march attracted only about 2,000 participants and a raft of protesters, a recent rally drew an estimated 75,000 people, both gay and straight, to walk together in solidarity. Seattle's established gay and lesbian bars include Neighbours (✉ 1509 Broadway ☎ 206/324–5358) and Wildrose (✉ 1021 E Pike ☎ 206/324–9210). The *Seattle Gay News* is a good local source of information.

### FADO IRISH PUB
Step back in time at this fine, atmospheric pub, hand-crafted in Ireland and transported to Seattle. Sup a pint of Guinness while listening to a live band or Irish fiddle music.
✚ G6 ✉ 801 1st Avenue ☎ 206/264–2700 ◷ Daily 11.30–2am

### FIRESIDE ROOM
With its overstuffed chairs and fireplace, this spot in the stately Sorrento Hotel takes you back to earlier, more genteel times.
✚ F6 ✉ 900 Madison Street ☎ 206/622–6400

### FX MCRORY'S STEAK CHOP & OYSTER HOUSE
With a first-rate oyster bar, more than 140 bourbons and 26 beers on tap, this sparkling brass-and-wood haunt across from the Kingdome attracts both professional athletes and sports fans. Full noisy bar.
✚ G6 ✉ 419 Occidental Avenue S ☎ 206/623–4800 ◷ Till midnight

### HARBOUR PUBLIC HOUSE
Neighborhood pub just a short walk from the ferry dock. Good burgers, fish'n'chips and pasta.
✚ Off map ✉ 231 Parfitt Way SW on Bainbridge Island ☎ 206/842–0969

### KELL'S IRISH RESTAURANT & PUB
The elegance of a Dublin supper room and the warmth of an Irish pub. Irish music.
✚ F5 ✉ 1916 Post Alley ☎ 206/728–1916

### LITTLE RED HEN
A genuine country and western bar in the Green Lake neighborhood. Live country music, line dancing, karaoke, beer and snacks. Hunker down for an early morning breakfast of chicken fried steak.
✚ A5 ✉ 7115 Woodlawn Avenue NE ☎ 206/522–1168 ◷ Mon–Fri 6am–2am, Sat 8am–2am, Sun 9am–2am

### THE PIKE PUB & BREWERY
Popular for its good food, excellent craft beers and affordable prices.
✚ F5 ✉ 1415 1st Avenue (in the Market) ☎ 206/622–6044 ◷ Till midnight

### QUEEN CITY GRILL
Belltown's classiest pub. The first-rate kitchen specializes in grilled entrées. Crowded and noisy.
✚ E5 ✉ 2201 1st Avenue ☎ 206/443–0975

### VIRGINIA INN
A Seattle institution. Art on the walls and a posted quotation providing food for thought for an eclectic group of patrons.
✚ E5 ✉ 1937 1st Avenue ☎ 206/728–1937 ◷ Mon–Thu 11am– midnight, Fri–Sat 11am–2am, Sun noon–midnight

### VON'S GRAND CITY CAFÉ
The city's best martini "or your money back." Prime rib and fruitwood-smoked turkey stand out in this dark wood haunt papered with cartoons, quirky memorabilia, photographs and quotes.
✚ E6 ✉ 619 Pine St ☎ 206/621–8667

# Spectator Sports Venues

### BASEBALL

The Seattle Mariners play at Safeco Field, the "state-of-the-art" ballpark that opened in 1999. The open-air stadium seats 47,000 and has a retractable roof that can be closed in bad weather. Baseball season runs from spring into fall; Safeco tours are available year round.

✚ F3 ✉ 1250 1st Avenue S at Royal Brougham
☎ 206/346–4287 for tickets; www.seattlemariners.com

### BASKETBALL

The Seattle SuperSonics, the city's oldest professional sports franchise, play at home in Key Arena October to April.

✚ D2 ✉ 1st Avenue N at Seattle Center
☎ 206/628–0888 (Ticketmaster); www.sonics.nba.com/sonics ▣ 1, 2, 13

The Seattle Storm is the city's newest professional sports team. A member of the WNBA, this women's team plays in Key Arena from the end of May through the middle of August.

✚ D2 ✉ 1st Avenue N at Seattle Center
☎ 206/628–0888 (Tickemaster)

### FOOTBALL

Seattle's NFL team, the Seahawks, play September through December in the new, 67,000-seat Seahawks Stadium located south of Pioneeer Square.

✚ A5 ☎ 1–888/NFL-HAWK; www.seahawks.com ▣ 71, 72, 73, 43, 25

The University of Washington's Huskies play PAC-10 football in fall at the Husky Stadium. Games are on Saturday.

✚ A5 ✉ Montlake Boulevard NE ☎ 206/543–2200

### HOCKEY

The WHL's Seattle Thunderbirds play in Key Arena September to May.

✚ D2 ✉ 400 1st Avenue N
☎ 206/448–7825;
www.seattle-thunderbirds.com
▣ 1, 2, 13, 15, 18

### HORSE-RACING

Emerald Downs, Auburn. Thoroughbred racing from March through September. Special events in summer.

✚ N3 ✉ 2300 Emerald Downs Drive, Auburn
☎ 1–888/931–8400;
www.emeralddowns.com
🕐 First race weekdays at 5pm, weekends and holidays at 1pm

### HYDROPLANE RACES

Held every August since 1950 on a 2-mile (3-km) course south of the Lake Washington floating bridge.

✚ Off map ☎ 206/728–0123 for viewing area tickets

### SOCCER

The Seattle Sounders, the city's professional men's soccer team, play at the Seahawks Stadium. Season runs April to October.

✚ B3 ✉ 5th Avenue N
☎ 1–800/796–KICK;
www.seattlesounders.net ▣ 1, 2, 15, 18

### TICKETMASTER

Tickets to many of Seattle's sporting events, as well as concerts, are available from this outlet.
☎ 206/628–0888

### DID YOU KNOW?

After speculation that the Seattle Seahawks football team would leave Seattle, billionaire Paul Allen, co-founder of Microsoft, stepped to the plate in 1997 and bought the team. The following summer, Seattle voters approved a referendum to tear down the massive Kingdome and build a new open-air stadium and exhibition center on its site. The new facility, which opened in summer 2002, is home to both the Seahawks pro-football and Seattle Sounder pro-soccer teams.

# Luxury Hotels

Expect to pay the following per night for a double room:

$ = under $85
$$ = $85–150
$$$ = Over $150

## DISCOUNTS AND PROMOTIONS

Many of the larger hotels and some smaller ones offer special corporate rates or discounts. Some hotels catering to business travelers may have reduced rates at weekends; in addition, most establishments lower their rates in the off-season.

### ALEXIS HOTEL ($$$)

Small downtown hotel with tasteful postmodern styling and impeccable service, 109 guest rooms.
✚ F6 ✉ 1007 1st Avenue ☎ 206/624–4844, 800/426–7033; fax 206/621–9009; www.alexishotel.com

### FOUR SEASONS OLYMPIC HOTEL ($$$)

Many consider this elegant 450-room hotel Seattle's finest. Built in 1924, it features a fitness center, pool, shops and several restaurants, including the lavish Georgian Room.
✚ F6 ✉ 411 University Street ☎ 206/621–1700, 800/819–5033; www.fourseasons.com

### HOTEL MONACO ($$$)

Lively and stylish hotel with personable staff and a fun restaurant—Sazerac. Some of the 189 rooms have two-person soaking tubs. Pet friendly.
✚ F6 ✉ 1101 4th Avenue ☎ 206/621–1770, 800/715–6513; fax: 206/624–0060; www.monaco-seattle.com

### INN AT HARBOR STEPS ($$$)

Elegant retreat near the waterfront. The 20 rooms are well-appointed. Spa fitness center and pool.
✚ F6 ✉ 1221 1st Avenue ☎ 206/748–0973, 888/728–8910; fax 206/748–0533; www.foursisters.com

### INN AT THE MARKET ($$$)

This charming 70-room hotel with French provincial decor shares a brick courtyard with Campagne Restaurant. Courtesy car.
✚ F5 ✉ 86 Pine Street ☎ 206/443–3600, 1–800/446–4484; fax: 206/448–0631; www.innatthemarket.com

### MAYFLOWER PARK ($$–$$$)

An elegant hotel with 172 rooms in a renovated 1920s building near Westlake Center. Home of the romantic Andaluca Restaurant.
✚ E5 ✉ 405 Olive Way ☎ 206/623–8700, 800/426–5100; fax: 206/382–6996; www.mayflower.com

### RESIDENCE INN BY MARRIOTT-LAKE UNION ($$$)

The 234 well-appointed rooms have fully-equipped kitchens and living rooms. Fitness center and pool. Pets allowed.
✚ C4 ✉ 800 Faiview Avenue N ☎ 206/624–6000, 800/331–3131; fax 206/223–8160; www.residenceinn.com/seattle

### SHERATON SEATTLE HOTEL & TOWERS ($$$)

Downtown tower with a striking lobby and 840 luxury rooms filled with art by Northwest artists. Health club and Fullers Restaurant.
✚ E6 ✉ 1400 6th Avenue ☎ 206/621–9000; fax 206/621–8441; www.sheraton.com/seattle

### WESTIN SEATTLE ($$$)

Large downtown hotel with an attractive lobby and fine bell staff; 865 rooms. Fitness center and Nikko's Restaurant. In-room modem hook-ups. Small pets allowed.
✚ E5 ✉ 1900 5th Avenue at Stewart ☎ 206/728–1000, 800/WESTIN–1; fax: 206/728–2259; www.westin.com

# Mid-Range Hotels

### EXECUTIVE EXTENDED STAY ($$)

Furnished apartment suites near hospitals on south Capitol Hill. Units have kitchens, washer-dryer, telephones with private lines and data ports; fitness center, spa. Complimentary shuttle to downtown.
✚ D4 ✉ 300 10th Avenue ☎ 206/223–9300, 800/906–6226; fax: 206/233–0241; www.executiveextendedstay.com

### HAMPTON INN DOWNTOWN ($$)

This new motor inn at Seattle Center has an attractive lobby and 124 comfortable rooms. Continental breakfast, premium cable TV, 24-hour fitness room. Free parking. Excellent value.
✚ D3 ✉ 700 5th Avenue N ☎ 206/282–7700, 800/ HAMPTON; fax: 206/282–0899; www.hamptoninn.com ▣ 3, 4, 16; Monorail to downtown

### HAWTHORN INN AND SUITES ($$)

Between downtown and Seattle Center, this hotel has 72 rooms. Free local calls and free parking. Complimentary breakfast, sauna and spa, fitness room and free bike rental.
✚ D3 ✉ 2224 8th Avenue ☎ 206/624–6820, 800/437–4867

### HOTEL SEATTLE ($$)

Downtown hotel with 81 rooms, renovated in 1996. The restaurant/ lounge serves breakfast and lunch.
✚ F6 ✉ 315 Seneca ☎ 206/623–5110, 800/ 426–2439; fax: 206/623–5110

### SILVER CLOUD INN–LAKE UNION ($$)

Opened 2003, this inn has 184 well-appointed guest rooms featuring high-speed internet connection. Other facilities include compli-mentary breakfast and airport shuttle, a concierge service, outdoor pool, fitness room and sauna.
✚ D3 ✉ 1150 Fairview Avenue N ☎ 206/447–9500, 800/330–5812; fax 206/812–4900; www.silvercloud.com

### SILVER CLOUD INN–UNIVERSITY ($$)

This inn has 180 units with mini kitchens. Swimming pool, fitness center, complimentary continental breakfast; free local calls. University Village area.
✚ A6 ✉ 5036 25th Avenue NE ☎ 206/526–5200, 800/205–6940; www.scinns.com

### WATERTOWN HOTEL ($$)

This inviting small hotel within walking distance of the University offers attractive studios or suites with large bathrooms and internet access.
✚ A6 ✉ 4242 Roosevelt Way NE ☎ 206/826–4242, 866/944–4242; fax: 206/315–4242; www.watertownseattle.com

### WESTCOAST VANCE HOTEL ($$)

Lovingly restored hotel. The 165 rooms and baths are tiny but immaculate. Bar and restaurant on-site.
✚ E6 ✉ 620 Stewart Street ☎ 206/441–4200, 800/325–4000; fax: 206/441–8612; www.westcoasthotels.com/vance

### LODGING GUIDES AND SERVICES

• Seattle/King County Convention and Visitor's Bureau website (www.seeseattle.org) contains a lodging guide and online coupons that can be printed and used for discounted rates.

• A Pacific Reservation Service has a website at www.seattlebedandbreak-fast.com. Click on "What I really want is a place…" and then on "Inexpensive Rates" for several appealing lodging options in residential areas.

• Try calling the Seattle Hotel Hotline (☎ 1–800.535–7071) for help with last minute hotel reservations.

# Budget Accommodations

## BED-AND-BREAKFAST

### GASLIGHT INN ($–$$)

Lovingly restored turn-of-the-20th-century mansion and annex. Fifteen well-appointed rooms, charming courtyard with plantings and a small swimming pool.

✚ D5 ✉ 1727 15th Avenue
☎ 206/325–3654;
www.gaslight-inn.com
▣ 10, 43

### INN AT QUEEN ANNE ($–$$)

Comfortable 68-room inn located in an older brick building next to Seattle Center. Complimentary breakfast, kitchenettes, cable TV, voicemail and air-conditioning.

✚ C2 ✉ 505 1st Avenue N
☎ 206/282–7357,
800/952–5043;
www.innatqueenanne.com
▣ 1, 2, 13, 15, 18

### SALISBURY HOUSE ($–$$)

Charming, beautifully restored and decorated 1904 home on a residential street on north Capitol Hill. A little gem with only five guest rooms

✚ C5 ✉ 750 16th Avenue E
☎ 206/328–8682;
fax: 206/ 720–1019;
www.salisburyhouse.com
▣ 10

## HOTELS

### ACE HOTEL ($)

This affordable and stylish Belltown hotel features futuristic lines in its 28 white-washed rooms, each with high ceilings, hardwood floors and a sink and vanity; some with private bathrooms. Attracts a hip clientele.

✚ D3 ✉ 2423 1st Avenue
☎ 206/448–4721

### COLLEGE INN GUEST HOUSE ($)

The upper floors of this 1904 Tudor building house a pension with 25 rooms, each with a bed, wash basin, writing desk and chair and shared bathroom. Bountiful continental breakfast. Café and pub downstairs.

✚ A5 ✉ 4000 University Way
NE ☎ 206/633–4441;
www.collegeinnseattle.com

### KINGS INN ($$)

Friendly staff, 68 rooms, and a great downtown location across from the monorail. Cable TV, laundry. Free parking.

✚ E5 ✉ 2106 5th Avenue
☎ 800/546–4760;
fax: 206/441–0730;
www.kingsinnseattle.com

### UNIVERSITY MOTEL ($)

Large suites on a quiet street in the University district. Twenty-one units with separate bedrooms, kitchens, pullout bed in living room and cable TV. Plain, dated furnishings, but plenty of room to swing a cat. Laundry; free parking. Per person charge.

✚ A6 ✉ 4731 12th Avenue
NE ☎ 206/522–4724,
800/522–4720

## HOSTELS

### GREEN TORTOISE HOSTEL ($)

At the Pike Place Market. Thirty-seven rooms, shared and private; linen provided. Shared kitchen, and common room with stereo, TV and VCR; lockers and laundry facilities. Free internet service, free breakfast, area discount card, 24-hour check-in.

✚ F5 ✉ 1525 2nd Avenue
☎ 206/340–1222, 888/
424–6783; www.greentortoise.
net; fax: 206/623–3207
▣ Free bus zone

### HOSTELLING INTERNATIONAL SEATTLE ($)

Bunkrooms for 4–6 people for a total of 139 beds; bedding included. Some private and family rooms; ample shared kitchen and common room; library with travel books and other resources. Non-members welcome but AYH members are given priority in busy seasons. Accessible for guests with disabilities.

✚ F5 ✉ 84 Union Street (1st-Western) ☎ 206/622–5443,
888/622–5443;
www.hiseattle.org

### YWCA ($)

Good central downtown location for women only. Twenty rooms with refrigerators, singles and doubles, some with private baths.

✚ F6 ✉ 1118 5th Avenue
☎ 206/461–4888; fax 206/
461–4860; www.ywcaworks.org

# **SEATTLE**
## travel facts

## ESSENTIAL FACTS

### Car Rental

- If you intend to rent a car and are not a US citizen, plan to bring your foreign licence and an international driver's licence, which must be acquired before arriving. Most car rental agencies require a major credit card; many will not rent a car to persons under 25.

### Customs regulations

- Duty-free allowances include 1 liter of alcoholic spirits or wine (no one under 21 may bring in alcohol), 200 cigarettes or 50 cigars (not Cuban) and up to $100-worth of gifts.
- Some medications may be prescription-only in the US and may be confiscated. Bring a doctor's certificate for essential medication.

### Discounts

- Ticket/Ticket: Half-price day-of-show tickets (cash only)—theater, concert, dance, comedy and music available at two locations: Pike Place Market Info Booth ✉ 1st and Pike and Broadway Market, 401 Broadway E on Capitol Hill ☎ 206/324–2744 ⊙ Closed Mon
- A CityPass ticket book will reduce admission prices by 50 percent to Woodland Park Zoo, Seattle Art Musum, Space Needle, Pacific Science Center, Seattle Aquarium and Museum of Flight. Passbooks can be purchased at any of the six attractions and are valid for seven days.
- Student travelers are advised to bring a current student ID to obtain discounted admissions.

### Electricity

- 110 volts, 60 cycles AC current.
- Electrical outlets are for flat, two-prong plugs. European appliances require an adaptor.

### Etiquette

- Seattle dress is informal; for most places, a jacket and tie are optional.
- Seattle has a successful recycling program. Many public places provide recycling bins. Littering is not tolerated.
- Smoking is prohibited in public places.
- Tipping 15–20 percent is customary in restaurants; 15 percent for taxis.

### Lavatories

- Public lavatories are located in Pike Place Market (base of the ramp in the Main Arcade) and in the Convention Center.

### Money matters

- Money-changing facilities are available at Sea-Tac Airport, banks and at Travelex Currency Service on level 3 of Westlake Center in downtown Seattle ☎ 206/682–4525
- Most major establishments and businesses accept major credit cards. Few places accept personal checks; bring travelers' checks.
- Automatic Teller Machines (ATMs) are available at most banks.

### Operating hours

- Banks: Generally Mon–Fri 9.30–5, some open Sat mornings.
- Offices: Normally Mon–Fri 9–5.
- Stores downtown open between 9–10am and typically close at 5–6pm with some staying open till 9 on Thursday evenings. Shops in shopping malls generally stay open Mon–Sat till 9pm; Sun till 5 or 6pm.

### National Holidays

New Year's Day (1 Jan); Martin Luther King Day (third Mon in

Jan); President's Day (third Mon in Feb); Memorial Day (last Mon in May); Independence Day (4 July); Labor Day (first Mon in Sep); Columbus Day (second Mon in Oct); Veterans' Day (11 Nov); Thanksgiving (fourth Thu in Nov); Christmas Day (25 Dec)

## Places of worship

Check the Yellow Pages of the phone book for complete listings. Some of the prominent houses of worship are listed below:

- Catholic: St. James Cathedral ☒ 9th and Marion ☎ 206/622–3559
- Congregational: Plymouth Congregational Church ☒ 6th and University ☎ 206/622–4865
- Episcopal: St. Marks Episcopal Cathedral ☒ 1245 10th Avenue E (Capitol Hill) ☎ 206/323–0300
- Greek Orthodox: St. Demetrios Greek Orthodox Church ☒ 2100 Boyer E ☎ 206/325–4347
- Lutheran: Gethsemane Lutheran Church ☒ 9th & Stewart ☎ 206/682–3620
- Methodist: First United Methodist ☒ 811 5th Avenue ☎ 206/622–7278
- Mosque: Islamic (Idriss) Mosque ☒ 1420 NE Northgate Way ☎ 206/363–3013
- Synagogues: Temple De Hirsch Sinai ☒ 1511 E Pike Street ☎ 206/323–8486

## Weights and measures

- Metric equivalents for US weights and measures are:
- Weights:
1 ounce (oz) = 28 grams; 1 pound (lb) = 0.45 kilogram;
1 quart (qt) = 0.9 liter (L).
- Measurements:
1 inch (") = 2.5 centimeters;
1 foot (') =0.3 meter;
1 yard (yd) = 0.9 meter;
1 mile = 1.6 kilometers.

## Visitor information

- Seattle-King County Convention and Visitors Bureau ☒ Level 1, Galleria/800 Convention Place in the Convention Center (8th and Pike) ☎ 206/461–5840; www.seeseattle.org 🕔 Mon–Fri 8.30–5, Sat 10–5 Memorial Day–Labor Day
- Seattle Center Info ☎ 206/684–7200; for recorded events information ☎ 206/684–8582
- Seattle Public Library offers a Quick Information number ☎ 206/386–4636. From June 2001, the downtown branch of the Seattle Public Library has been housed in a temporary home at 800 Pike Street, across from the Washington State Convention Center. A new library is projected to open in the spring of 2004 at 1000 4th Avenue between Spring and Madison.

## GETTING AROUND

### Bicycle

- The city has a number of bicycle routes. For bicycle rental, see Active Pursuits (► 58–59).

### Metro Buses

- For Metro Rider Information ☎ 206/553–3000 or 800/542–7876; also online information www.transit.metrokc
- The Metro tunnels under Pine Street and 3rd Avenue with five downtown stations: Convention Place, Westlake, University Street, Pioneer Square and the International District. All tunnel routes stop at each station. Sunday and evenings after hours when the tunnel is closed, tunnel buses run above ground along 3rd Avenue.
- Seattle bus drivers are not required to call out the stops along the route. Ask your driver to alert you once you have reached your stop.

## Monorail (► 7)

### Taxis

- The flag-drop charge is $1.80 and it's $1.80 for each additional mile.
- Major companies with 24-hour dispatch service include Yellow Cab, which has merged with Graytop Cab ☎ 206/622–6500 or 206/282–8222. Also FarWest ☎ 206/622–1717

### Washington State ferries

- Jumbo ferries from Seattle's downtown terminal to Bainbridge Island and Bremerton (on the Kitsap Peninsula) depart regularly from Colman Dock at pier 52. They take walk-on passengers and cars.
- Most ferry routes are very busy during weekday commute periods and on sunny weekends. Expect waits of two hours or more in summer and on holiday weekends.
- Schedules change seasonally; ☎ 206/464–6400 for information.
- Additional ferry routes departing from the Seattle environs serve the Kitsap Peninsula, Vashon Island, Whidbey Island, Port Townsend (Olympic Peninsula), the San Juan Islands, and Victoria, British Columbia.
- Credit cards are not accepted.
- Passengers to Canada need passports or other proof of citizenship.

### Waterfront streetcar

- A vintage 1927 trolley runs along the waterfront on Alaskan Way from pier 70 at Broad Street to 5th and Jackson in the International District with intermediate stops at Vine, Bell, Pike, University, Madison, Washington Streets and at Occidental Park in Pioneer Square.
- When you board, pay your fare and ask for a transfer, which is good for 90 minutes of sightseeing

before reboarding. Total ride, end to end, takes 20 minutes. Service every 20 minutes to half an hour, Mon–Fri 7–6, Sat–Sun 9.30–6 with extended summer hours.

### Community transit buses

- Bus service to points outside the city ☎ 800/562–1375
- For more information on getting around (► 7).

## MEDIA & COMMUNICATIONS

### Mail

- The main downtown post office is on the corner of Union and 3rd Avenue. Hours are Mon–Fri 8–5.30; closed Sat–Sun. Branch offices are located in most neighborhoods. ☎ 800/275–8777 for 24-hour infoline with Zip codes, postal rates, post office hours and location; or www.usps.com.
- Stamps can be bought at many supermarket check-out counters.

### Newspapers and magazines

- Seattle has two daily papers: *The Seattle Times* ☎ 206/464–2111 and the *Seattle Post-Intelligencer* ☎ 206/448–8000
- Weeklies with extensive entertainment listings include the alternative *Stranger* and *The Weekly*. Both are free.
- *The Seattle Gay News*—a community newspaper ☎ 206/324–4297
- International newspapers are sold at *First and Pike News* ✉ 93 Pike Street at the Pike Place Market and at *Bulldog News* ✉ 401 Broadway E

### Telephones

- To call Seattle from the UK dial 00 1(the code for US), followed by the area code , then the 7 digit number. To call the UK from

Seattle, dial 011 44 then drop the first zero from the area code.
- To make a local call from a pay phone, listen for a dial tone, then deposit coins; wait for new dial tone and dial the number.
- Phonecards for long-distance calls are available at most shops.
- To pay cash for long-distance calls, follow the same initial procedure as for local calls, and a recorded operator message will tell you how much additional money to deposit for the first three minutes; then deposit additional coins and dial.
- The area running east of Lake Washington from Everett to Maple Valley and east to Snoqualmie pass uses area code 425. The 253 area code runs south from Renton to the Pierce-Thurston county line. Other calls within western Washington require dialing a 360 area code.
- Directory assistance is a toll call. For information, dial 1 plus the area code plus the number plus the 555–1212.

## Television and Radio
- Seattle's two National Public Radio stations (NPR) are KUOW at 94.9 FM (all-talk radio with news from the BBC) and KPLU, an award-winning jazz station at 88.5 FM.
- KING-FM (98.1) Classical music.
- Seattle's six local television channels are: KOMO 4 (ABC); KING 5 (NBC); 7 (CBS); KCTS/9 (PBS); KSTW 11 (independent); and 13 (Fox).

## EMERGENCIES

### Consulates
- British ✉ 900 4th Avenue, suite 3001 ☎ 206/622–9255
- Canadian ✉ 412 Plaza 600, 6th Avenue &

Stewart Street ☎ 206/443–1777
- French ✉ 2200 Alaskan Way, suite 490 ☎ 206/256–6184
- Japanese ✉ 601 Union Street, suite 500 ☎ 206/682–9107

## Emergency phone numbers
- Police, ambulance or fire: ☎ 911
- The Red Cross Language Bank provides free, on-call interpretive assistance in emergency or crisis situations. Volunteers in over 60 languages. ☎ 206/323–2345

## Lost property
- Airport lost and found ☎ 206/433–5312
- King Street Station lost and found ☎ 206/382–4713; Metro bus lost and found ☎ 206/553–3090

## Medical treatment
- It is vital to have comprehensive insurance.
- US Healthworks operates several drop-in clinics; nearest clinic to downtown is the clinic at Denny and Fairview ☎ 206/682–7418 🕐 Mon–Fri 7am–6pm, Sat 9–3. Also at ✉ 8313 Aurora Avenue N ☎ 206/784–0737 🕐 Mon–Fri 8am–7pm, Sat 9am–5pm
- Dentist Referral Service ☎ 206/443–7607

- **24-hour pharmacies** Bartell Drug Store ✉ 600 1st Avenue N (near Seattle Center ☎ 206/284–1354)
- Walgreen Drug Store ✉ 5409 15th Avenue NW ☎ 206/781–0056

## Safety/crime
- Exercise caution and at night avoid the areas around 1st to 2nd and Pike, the edges of Pioneer Square, and the area between 2nd and 4th from Cherry to Yesler.
- Seattle police are well-known for ticketing jaywalkers.

# Index

# CityPack
## Seattle *Top 25*

### ABOUT THE AUTHOR
Suzanne Tedesko has lived in Seattle since 1975. Having travelled all over the world, she has written travel books on a range of subjects. She has also worked as an urban ethnographer and as a producer for film, television and radio.

| | |
|---|---|
| **WRITTEN BY** | Suzanne Tedesko |
| **EDITION REVISER** | Suzanne Tedesko |
| **MANAGING EDITORS** | Apostrophe S Limited |
| **COVER DESIGN** | Tigist Getachew, Fabrizio La Rocca |

A CIP catalogue record for this book is available from the British Library.

**ISBN 0 7495 4018 4**

The contents of this publication are believed correct at the time of printing. Nevertheless, the publishers cannot be held responsible for any errors or omissions or for changes in the details given in this guide or for the consequences of any reliance on the information provided by the same. This does not affect your statutory rights. Assessments of attractions, hotels, restaurants, and so forth are based upon the author's own personal experience and, therefore, descriptions given in this guide necessarily contain an element of subjective opinion which may not reflect the publishers' opinion or dictate a reader's own experiences on another occasion. We have tried to ensure accuracy in this guide, but things do change and we would be grateful if readers would advise us of any inaccuracies they may encounter.

Published by AA Publishing, a trading name of Automobile Association Developments Limited, whose registered office is Millstream, Maidenhead Road, Windsor, Berkshire, SL4 5GD. Registered number 1878835.

© **AUTOMOBILE ASSOCIATION DEVELOPMENTS LIMITED 1999, 2002, 2004**
First published 1999. Revised second edition 2002. Revised third edition 2004.

Colour separation by Daylight Colour Art Pte Ltd., Singapore
Printed and bound by Hang Tai D&P Limited, Hong Kong.

### ACKNOWLEDGMENTS
The Automobile Association would like to thank the following photographers, libraries and associations for their assistance in the preparation of this book.
The Boeing Company 50; Fifth Avenue Theatre (Dick Busher) 56; Frank O. Gehry & Associates Inc. (Joshua White) 33t; Museum of Flight 45t, 45b; Rex Features 33b; Seattle Municipal Archive 16c, 17c; Seattle Visitors and Convention Bureau 1, 9c, 10c, 11c, 12c, 14c, 15cr, 19t, 19cl, 21, 24cl; Stockbyte 5; University of Washington 46; Woodland Park Zoo (Renee de Martin) 30b
The remaining photographs are held in the Association's own library (AA WORLD TRAVEL LIBRARY) and were taken by JA Tims, with the exception of 13t which was taken by Harold Harris; and back cover; shopping bags, 20c which were taken by Clive Sawyer

A01600
Maps © Automobile Association Developments Limited 1999, 2002
Fold out map © Rand McNally 1998. R. L. #89–S–123
Transport map © TCS, Aldershot, England

### TITLES IN THE CITYPACK SERIES
• Amsterdam • Bangkok • Barcelona • Beijing • Berlin • Boston • Brussels & Bruges •
• Chicago • Dublin • Florence • Hong Kong • Lisbon • Ljubljana • London • Los Angeles •
• Madrid • Melbourne • Miami • Montréal • Munich • New York • Paris • Prague • Rome •
• San Francisco • Seattle • Shanghai • Singapore • Sydney • Tokyo • Toronto • Venice •
• Vienna • Washington •